# REALITY, CURATED

Valentina Loffredo

**COLLECTIVE SHORTS**
*by* NHP PUBLISHING

To Matteo and Azzurra

*As for me, I'm very little*

## Delicate Dissonances
Valentina Loffredo's Photography

In the creation of a surreal dimension, Valentina Loffredo embraces the interpretative audacity of an innovative language, which is itself a pure reflection of her thoughts and unique vision. The coordinates of real life and the usual methods to interpret images cannot unlock their secret. Only dreams and imagination can try to explain it from within. And, indeed, while creating a new perception, it is the author herself who dictates the rules of that amazing grammar of fantasy that sets the pace of a conscious stylistic choice.

On second thoughts, if we looked at these photographs with the eyes of the composition purists, we would have no chance to understand their message in depth. But if, instead, we decided to let our gaze roam over that particular kind of pleasure we feel in front of the sea under the August sun, then we would appreciate their profound sense of freedom and lightness.

What is needed is a radical change of perspective. Only a new angle of vision, free from formalism, can give access to the playful and spontaneous creativity that is implied in each image of "As For Me, I'm Very Little". In this regard, it is the author herself to give us the first important clue to her personal approach to photography. And she does so by revealing that the title of her series is not simply a concise indication of its content, but the acronym of her name: Very Little stands (also) for Valentina Loffredo. Little and tiny is, indeed, the figure of the author who, with wide eyes open, looks at the world with enchantment and delicate sensibility.

However, we cannot consider the autobiographical element as a simple point of view. It is rather a method for the visual perception, which produces a reversal of reality so bold to astonish during every moment of the artistic creation. Here then, the most important reference for the author's inspiration can be found in the purity of childhood, which, in turn, is translated into a reality dreamt with open eyes. This allows the discovery of the attractive and mysterious side of each thing and it creates the space where to fly with the wings of creativity.

There is no plausible logical explanation, as we attempt to read these images. What is great suddenly appears tiny; what is empty is filled with unexpected presences, and the colours are there to fill every surface. It is as if a visual short-circuit burst into the perfectly staged sets and, in one fell swoop, broke the geometry they are based upon.

Valentina Loffredo defines this creative process as a "celebration of possibilities." And possibilities, in fact, they are. Possibilities that break the monotony and the superficiality of the cliché in favour of a maverick dialectic that is not only appealing, but that suggests new horizons for the thought. Looking with attention at her work, there is always a detail out of place, a small coincidence of forms or visual allusions that offer an opportunity to go beyond the apparent rigidity.

"I choose a place that I find interesting and somehow familiar (pools, patterned walls, factory buildings) and I change it slightly, to build another one that is just the same, but for an element of surprise. [...] What I would like to convey is the grace we indulge in when we look beyond, when we expose ourselves to something that we had not considered, with curiosity and vulnerability."

The search for a meaning that lies beyond the surface is an endemic need that drives the aesthetic and stylistic values of Valentina Loffredo's out of stage photography. And her words seem pronounced specifically for this photographic series, which tell the story

of reality by transforming it, and make us doubt that what we are looking for, in reality, it is not as it appears.

In this sense, the surrealist inspiration is expressed with consistency both in the aesthetics and in the content. And, in particular, it recalls that eccentric personality which – within the avant-garde movements of the twentieth century – earned the nickname of le saboteur tranquille, just for his ability to insinuate doubts about reality through the representation of reality itself. René Magritte was not interested in reality to interpret it, nor to portray it, but to show its indefinable mystery. In this regard, in the prime of his painting production, he wrote: "Reality is never how we see it: the truth is, above all, imagination."

On the flowing rhythm of these words, "As For Me, I'm Very Little" reveals new discoveries and new ways of understanding life and the world. Therefore, the innocence of a gaze is not a perspective that only belongs to children. Now we can also share it, thanks to these images that become wonderful and delicate dissonances. An emotional renewed tradition of seeing, at last.

*Denis Curti – Photography Critic*

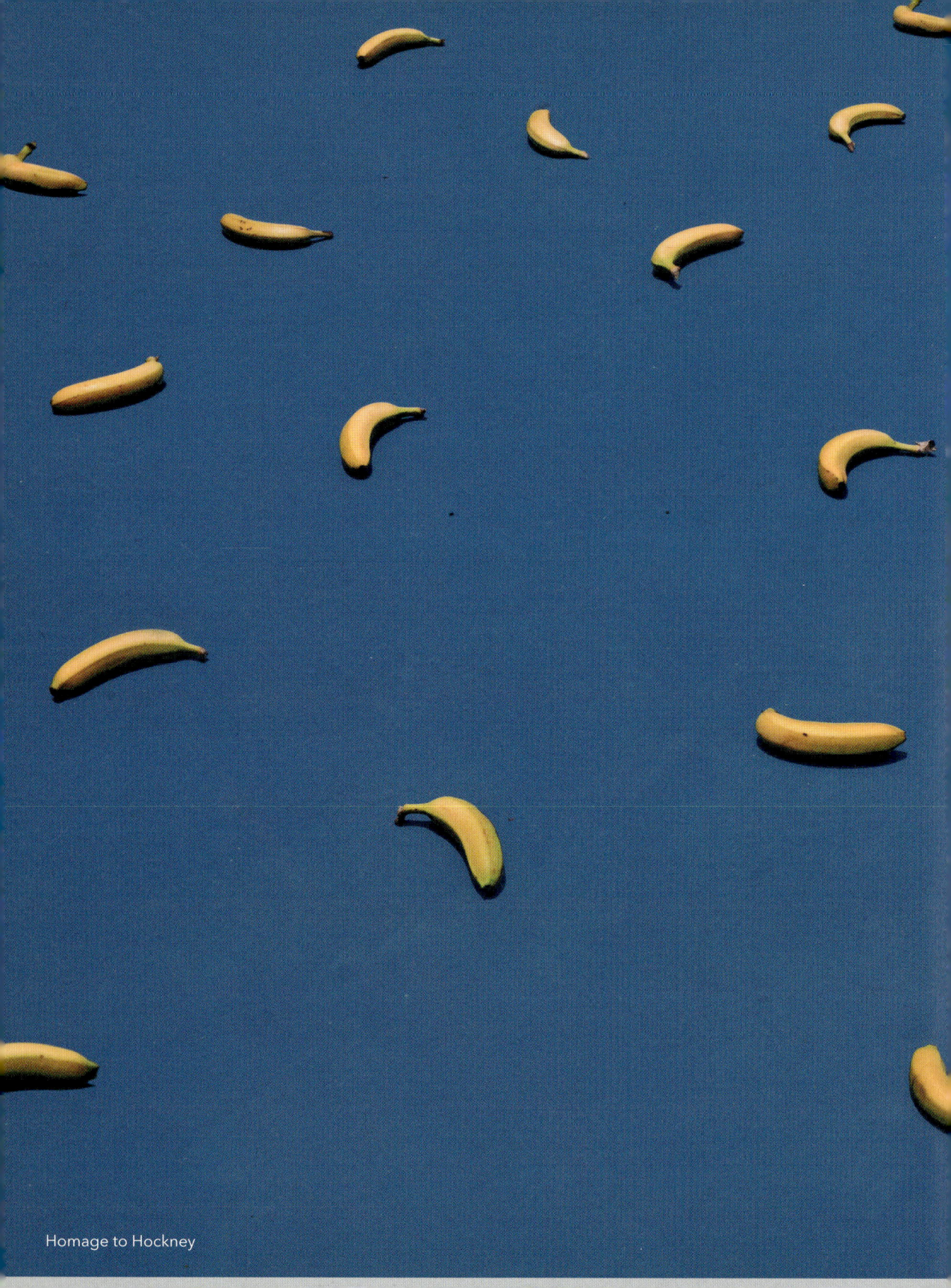

Homage to Hockney

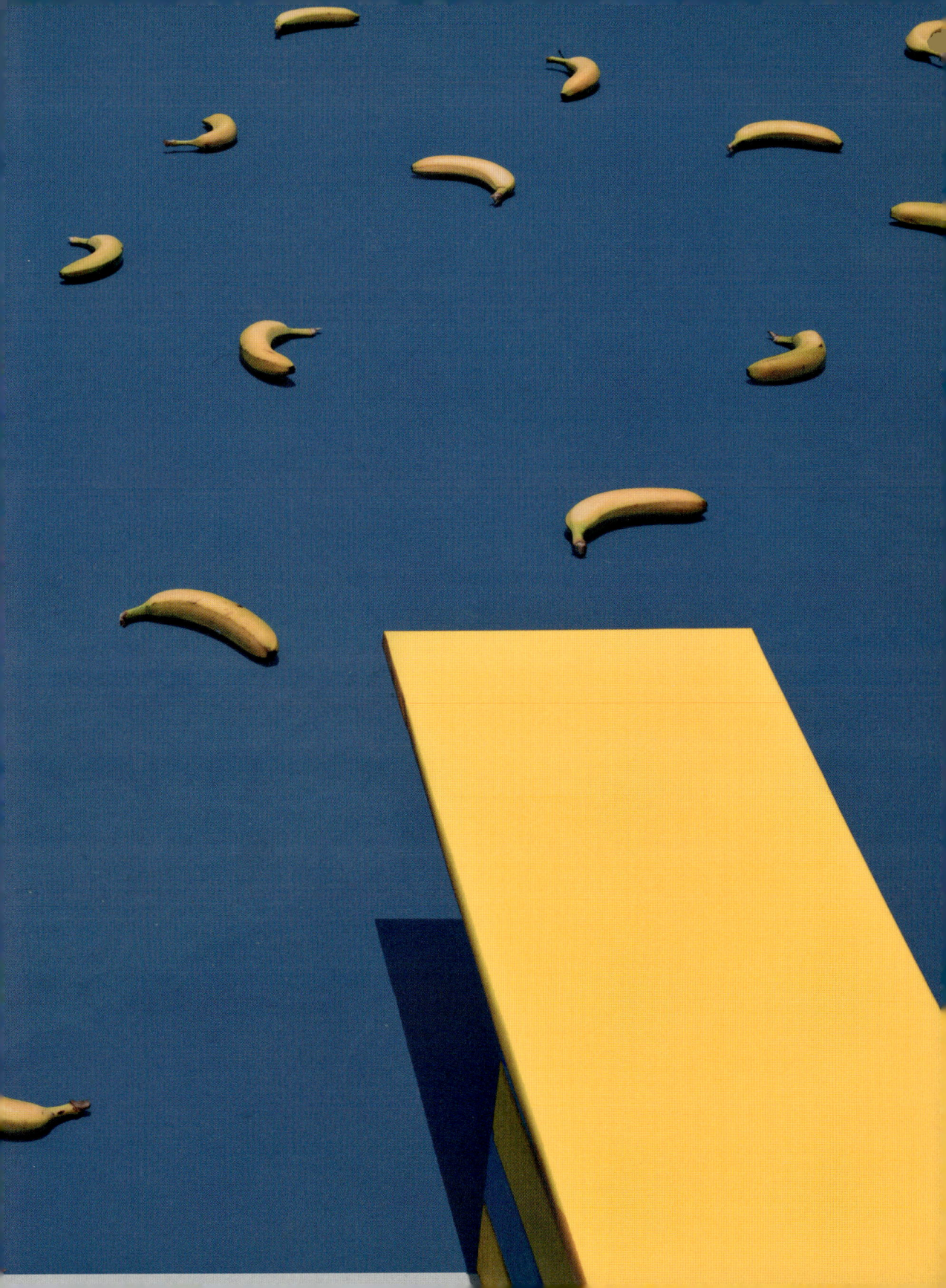

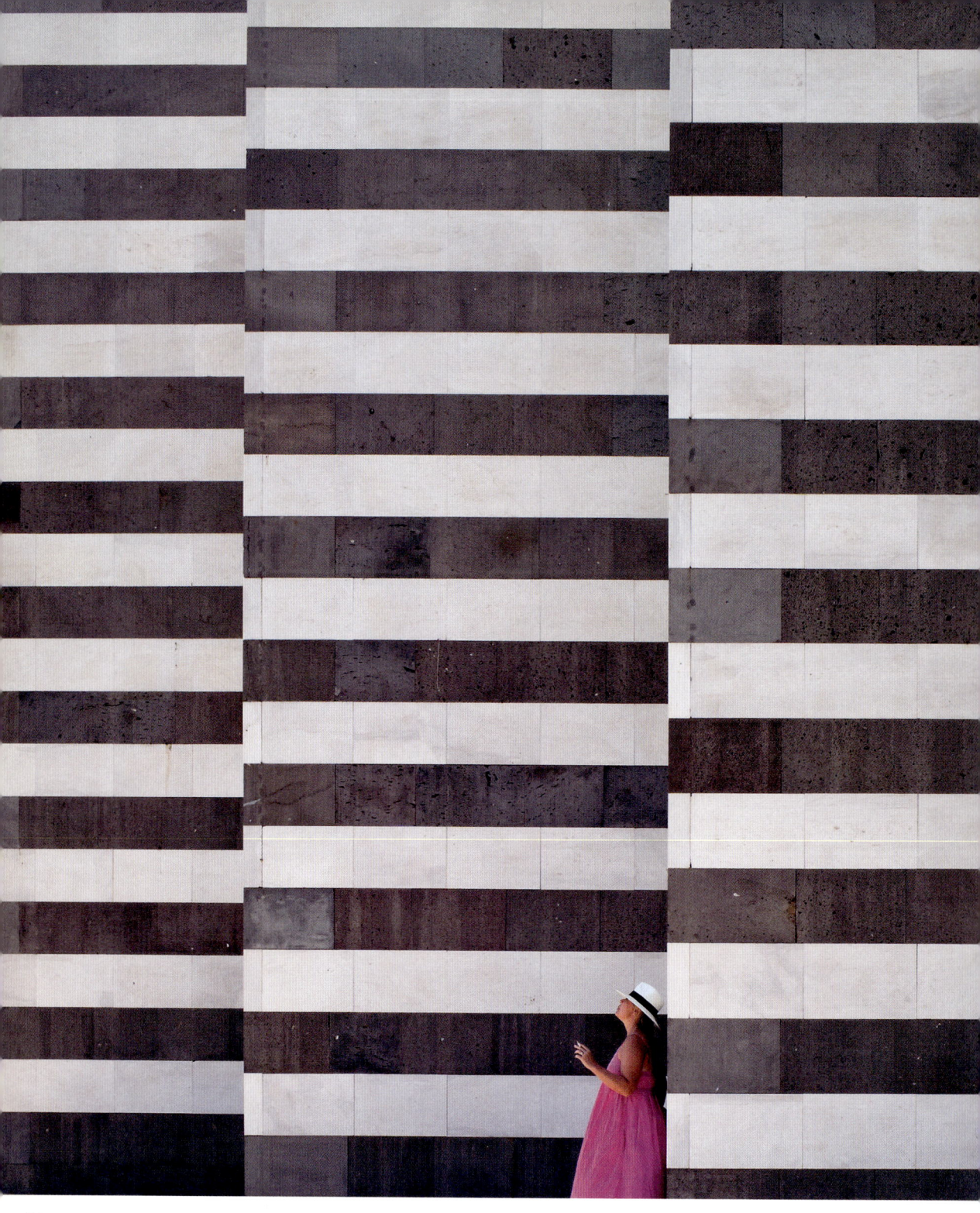

A true story

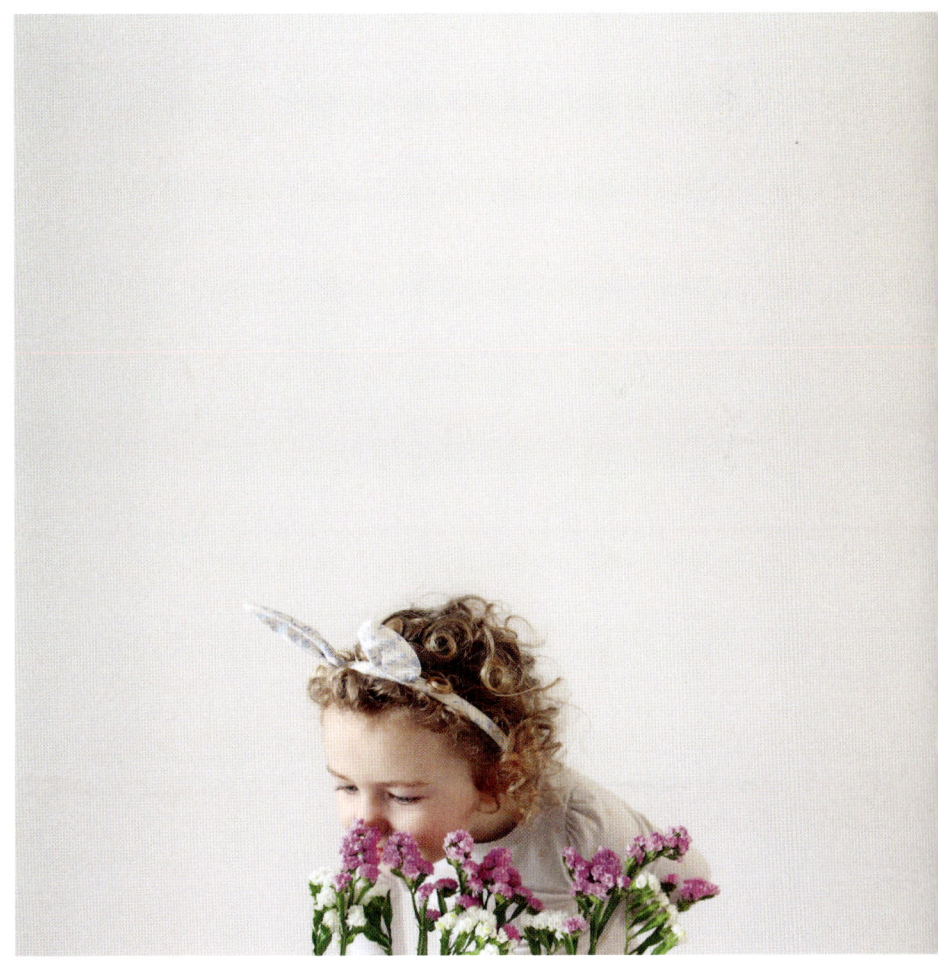

Bare necessities

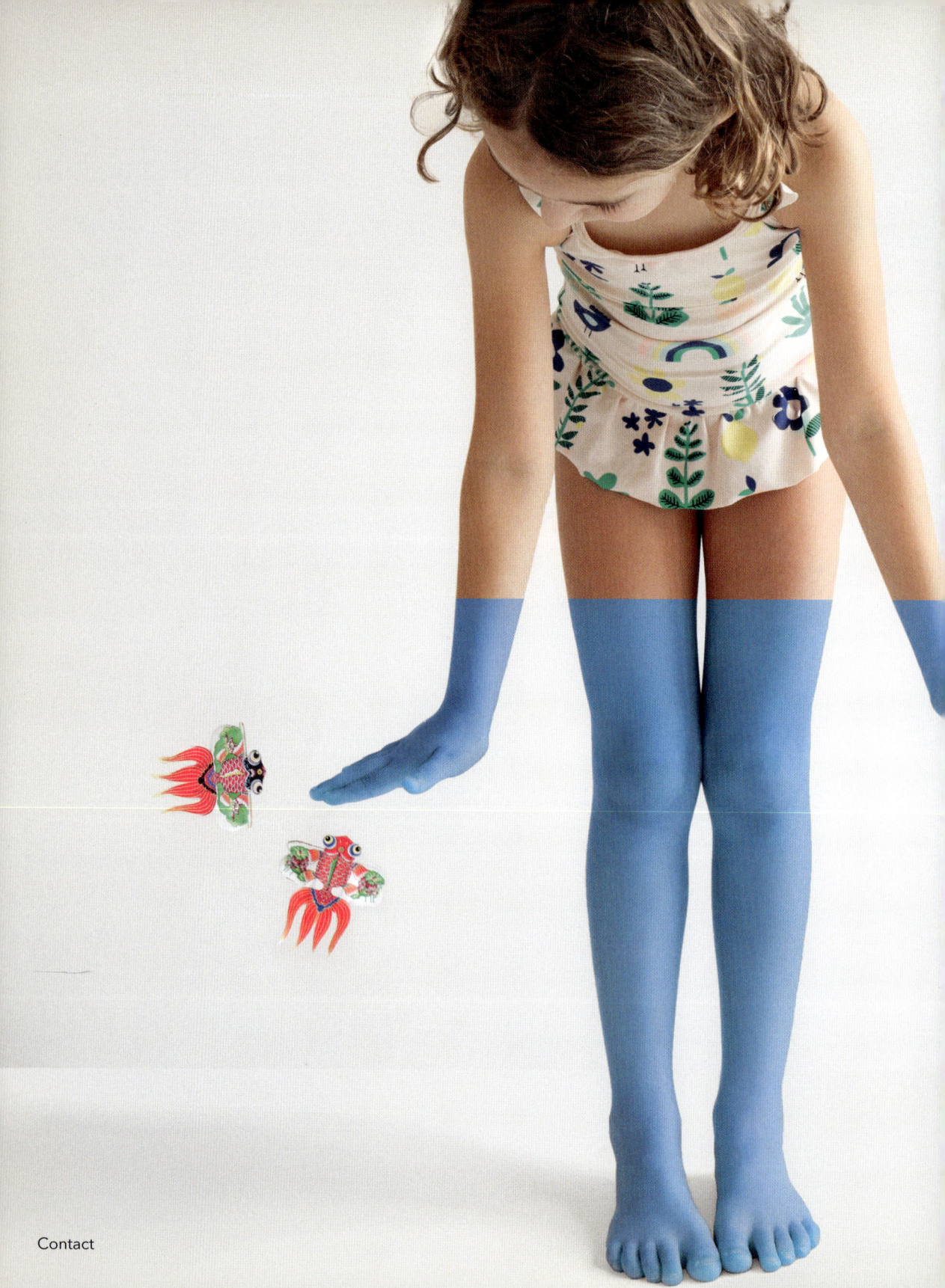

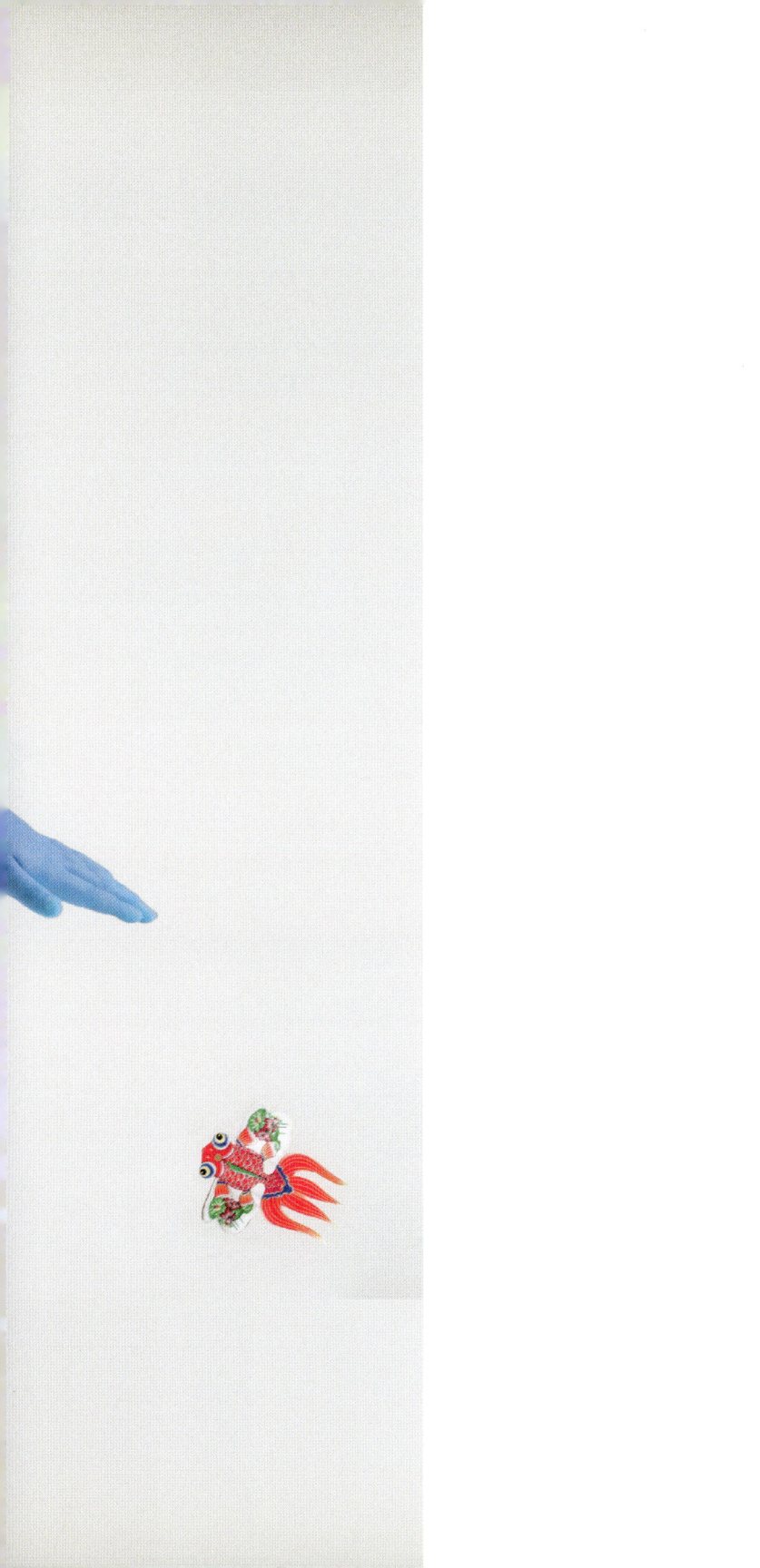

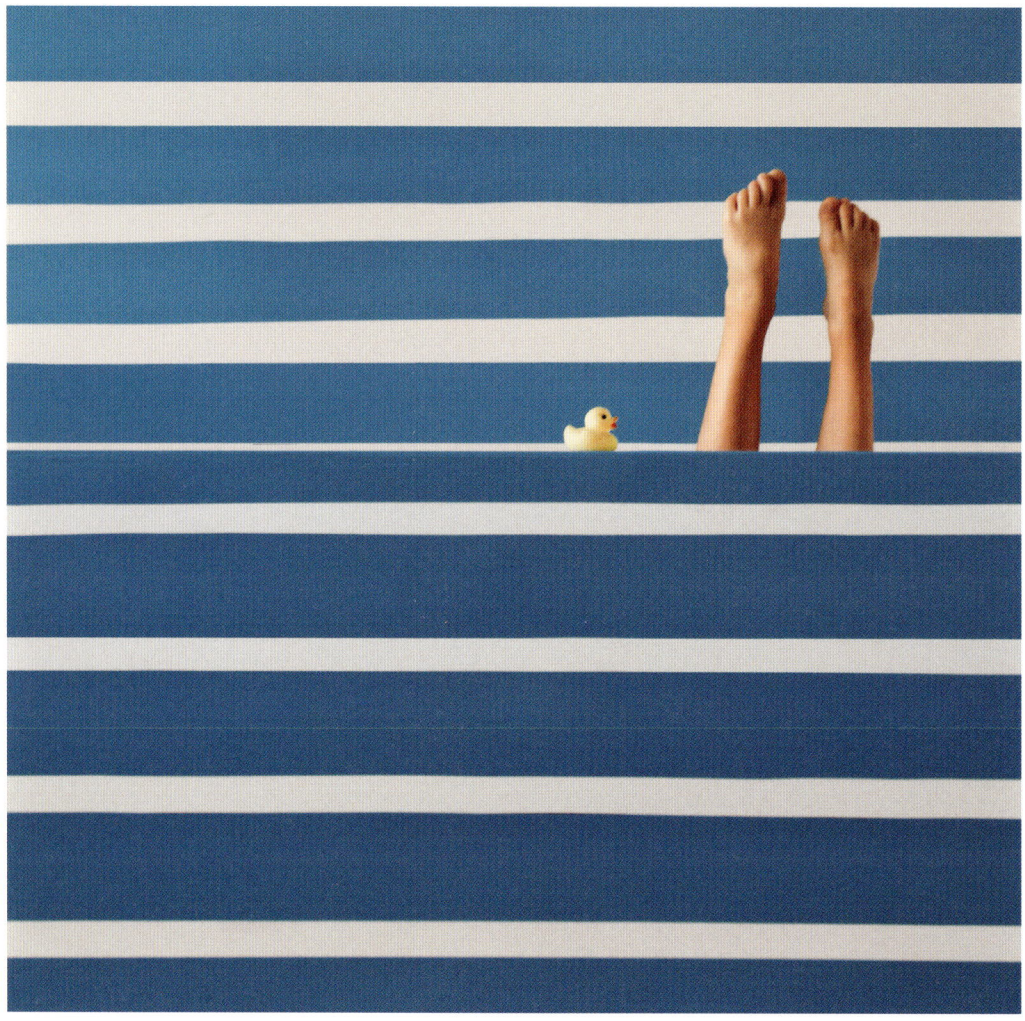

Dive in

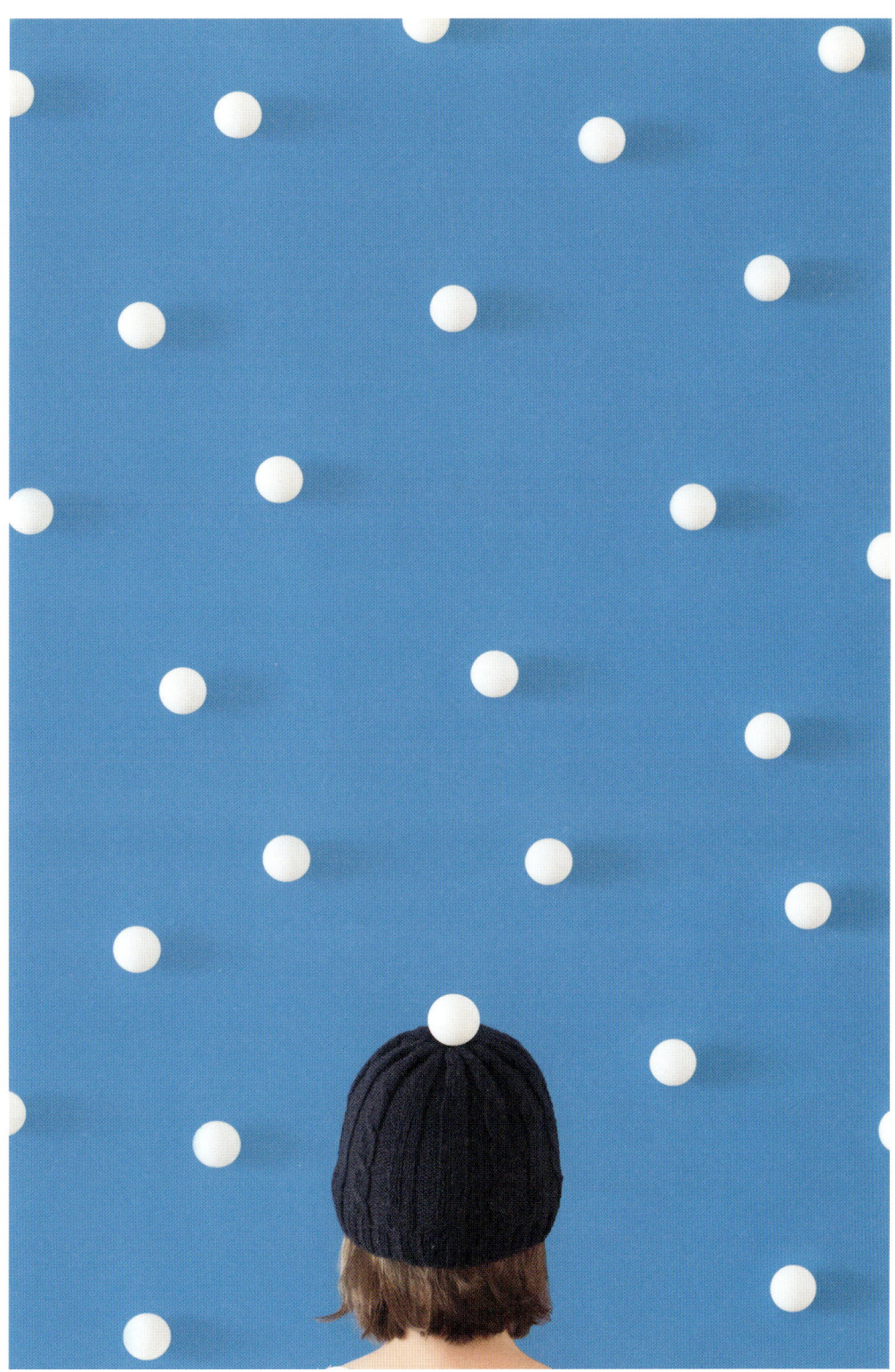

Up to snow good

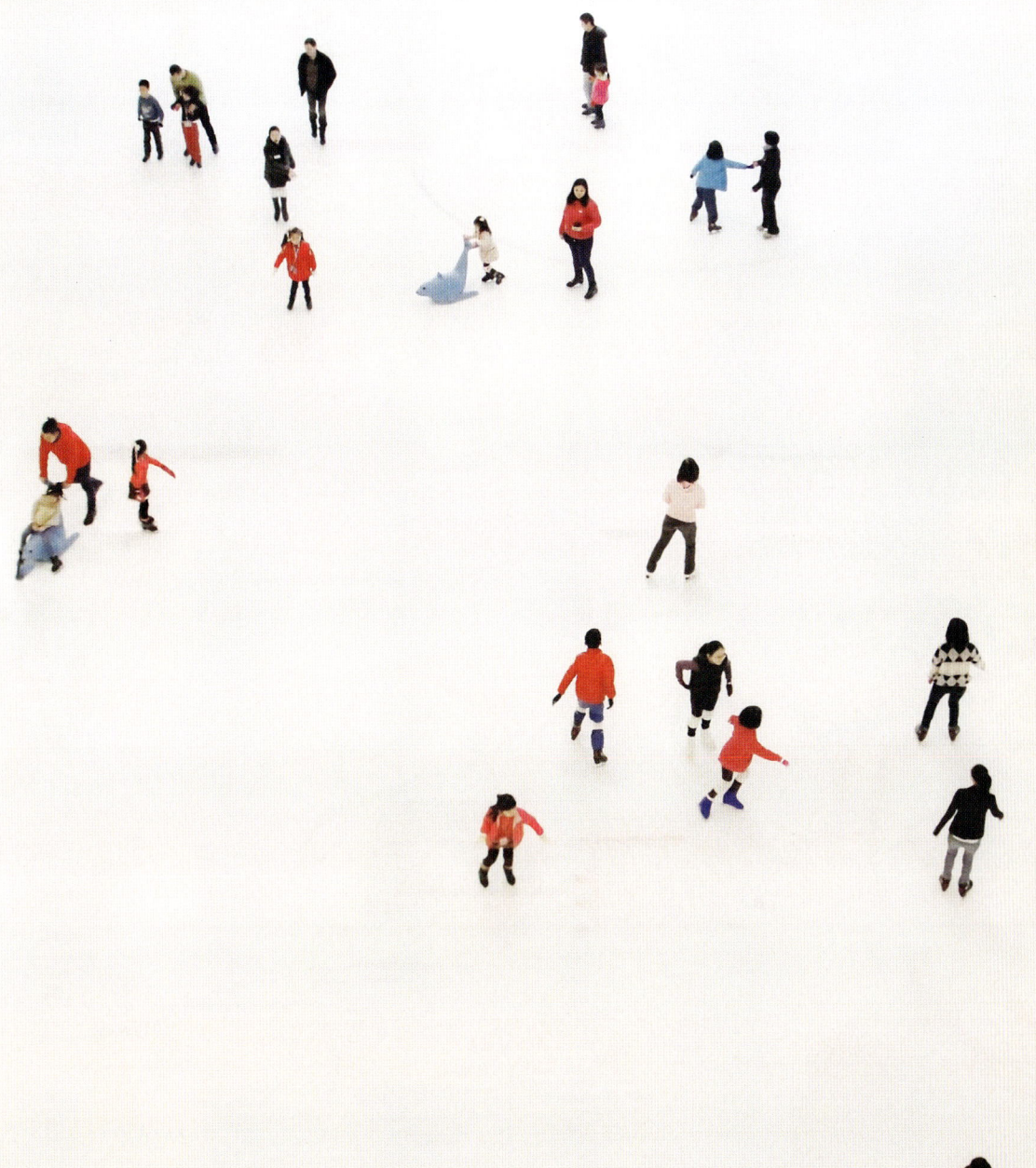

We all start as strangers

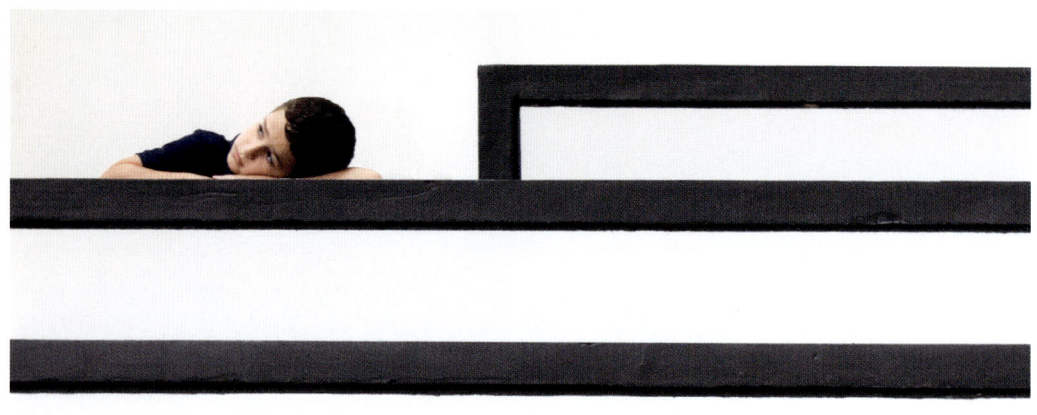

Acceptance

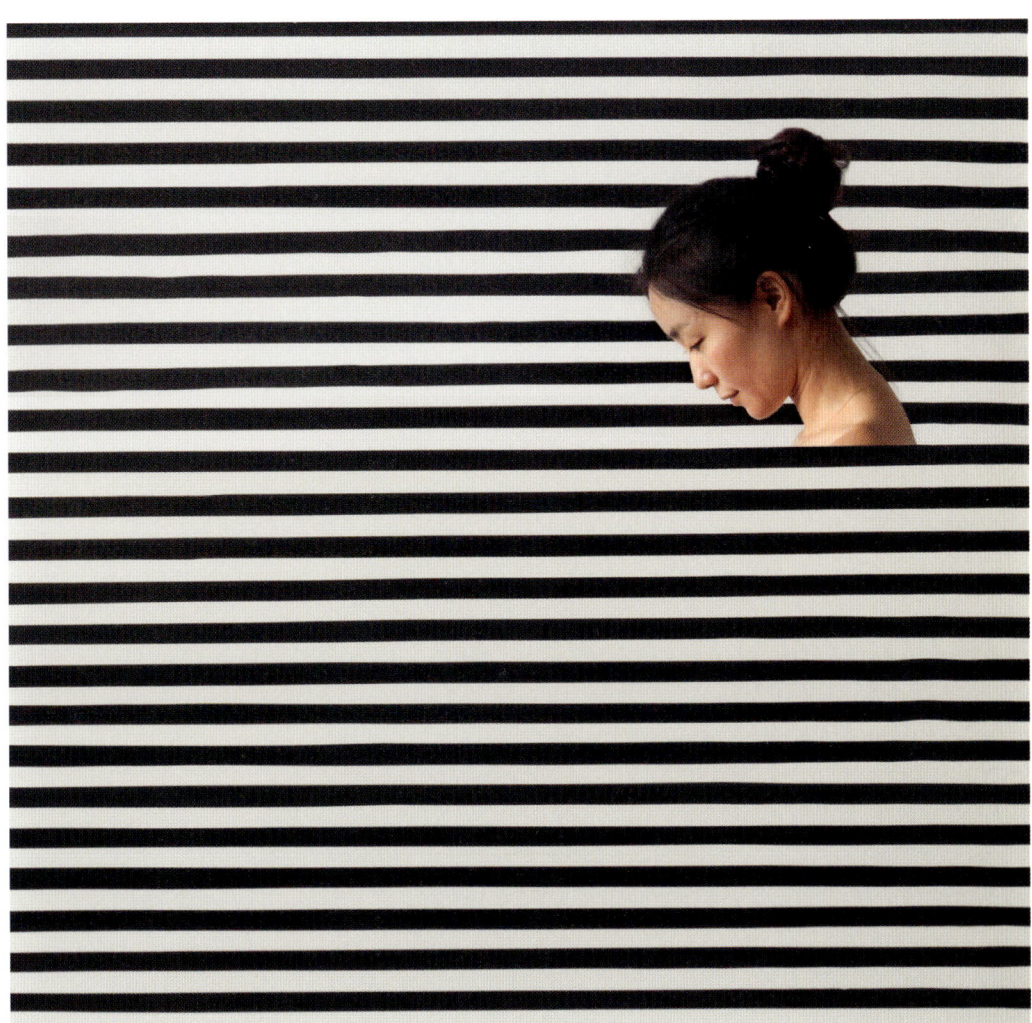

Stripe tease

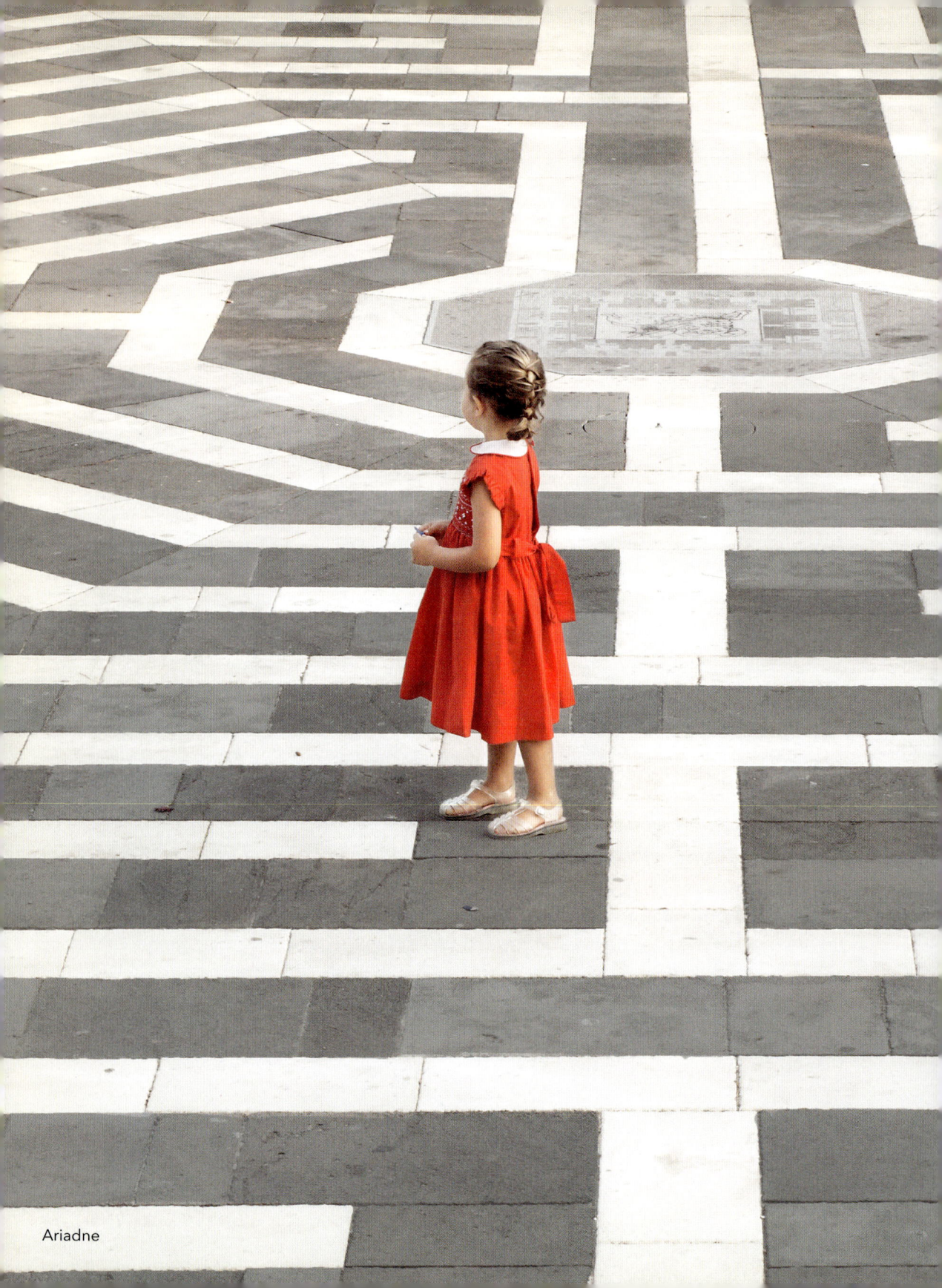

Ariadne

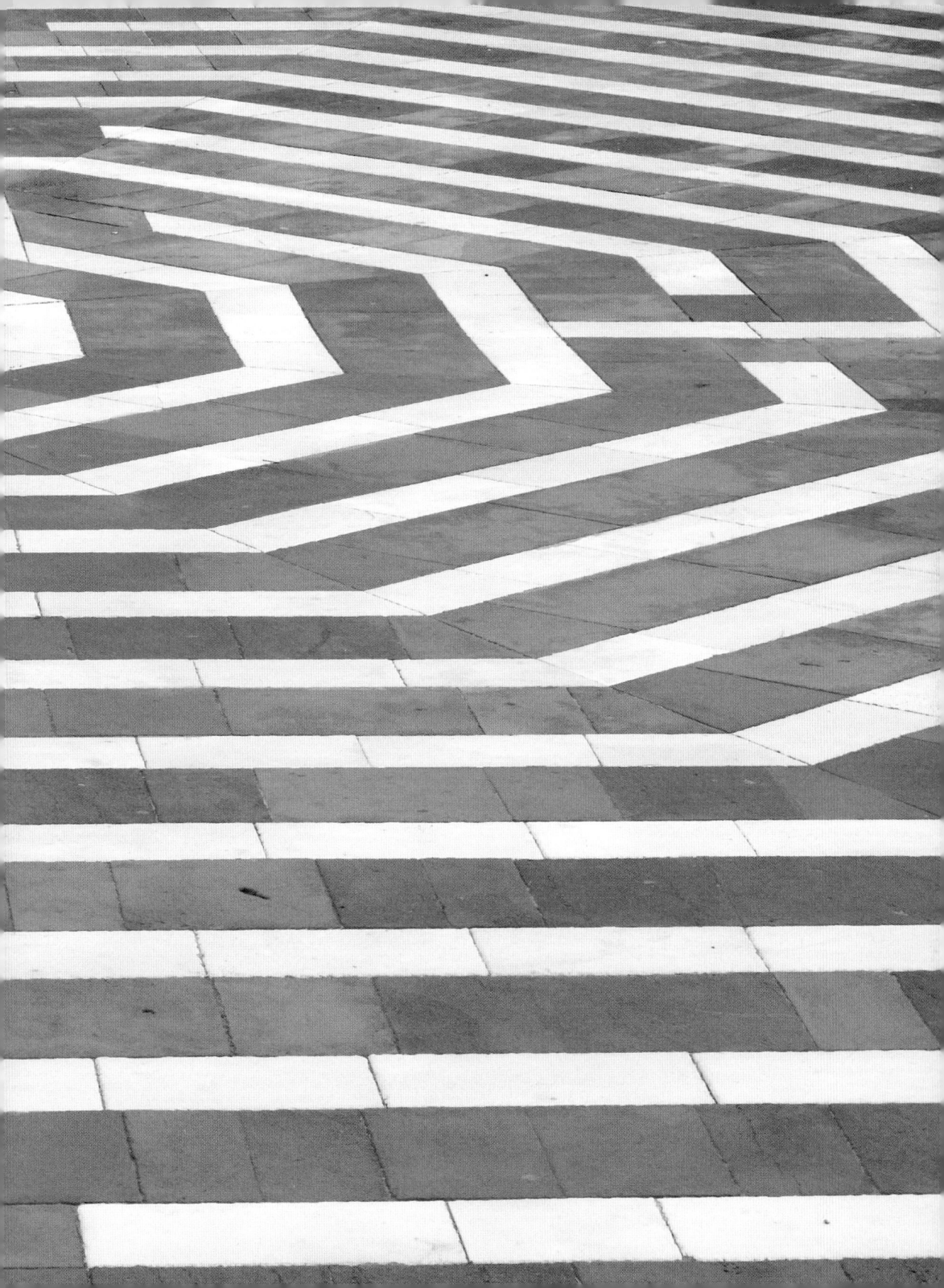

Flying by

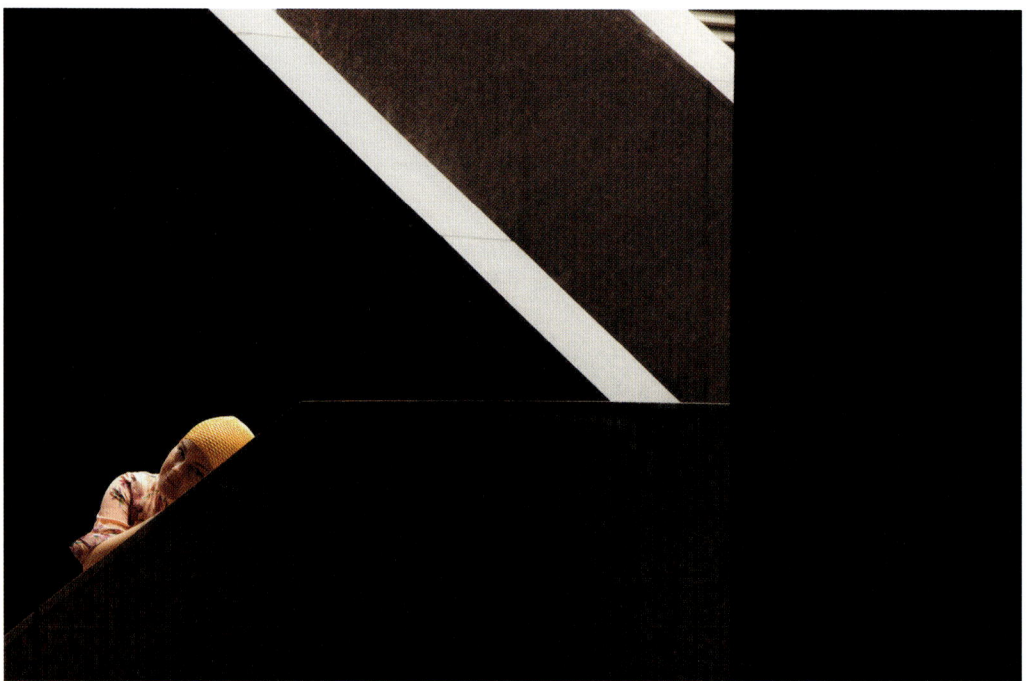

Handle with care

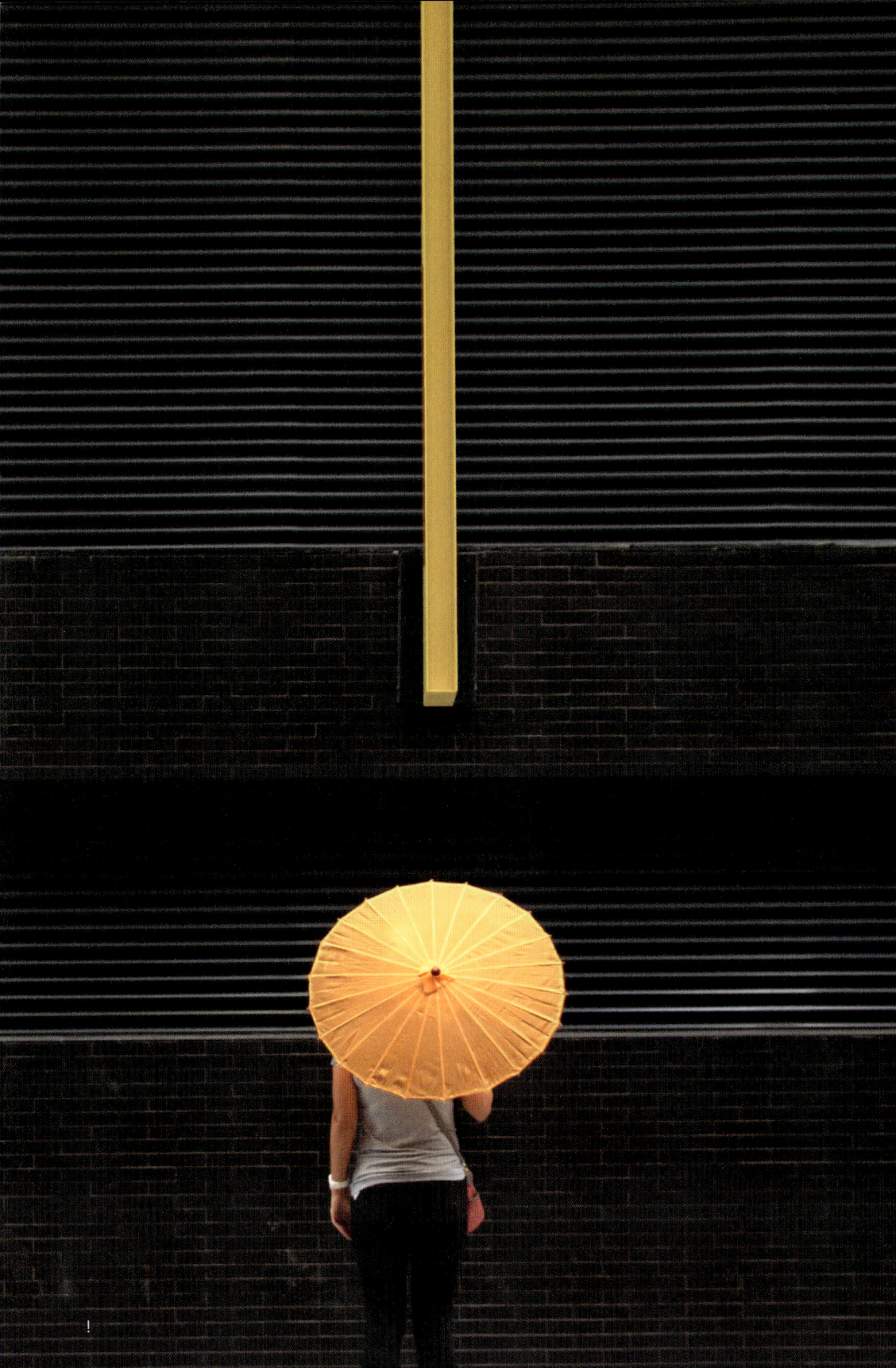

Trail

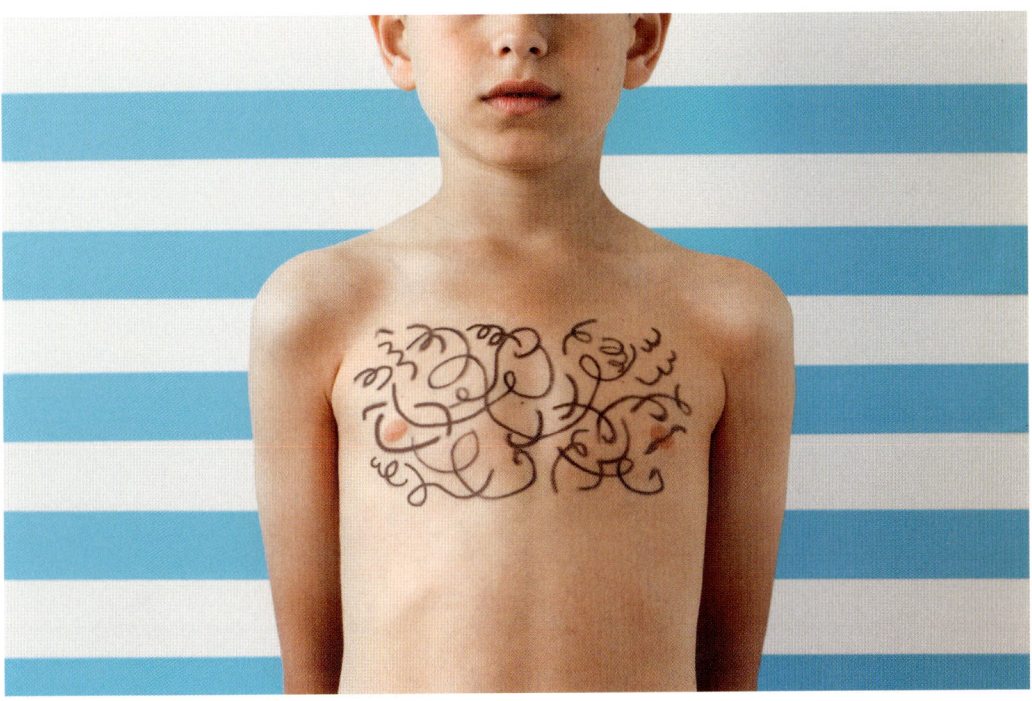

Ambitions

iLiner

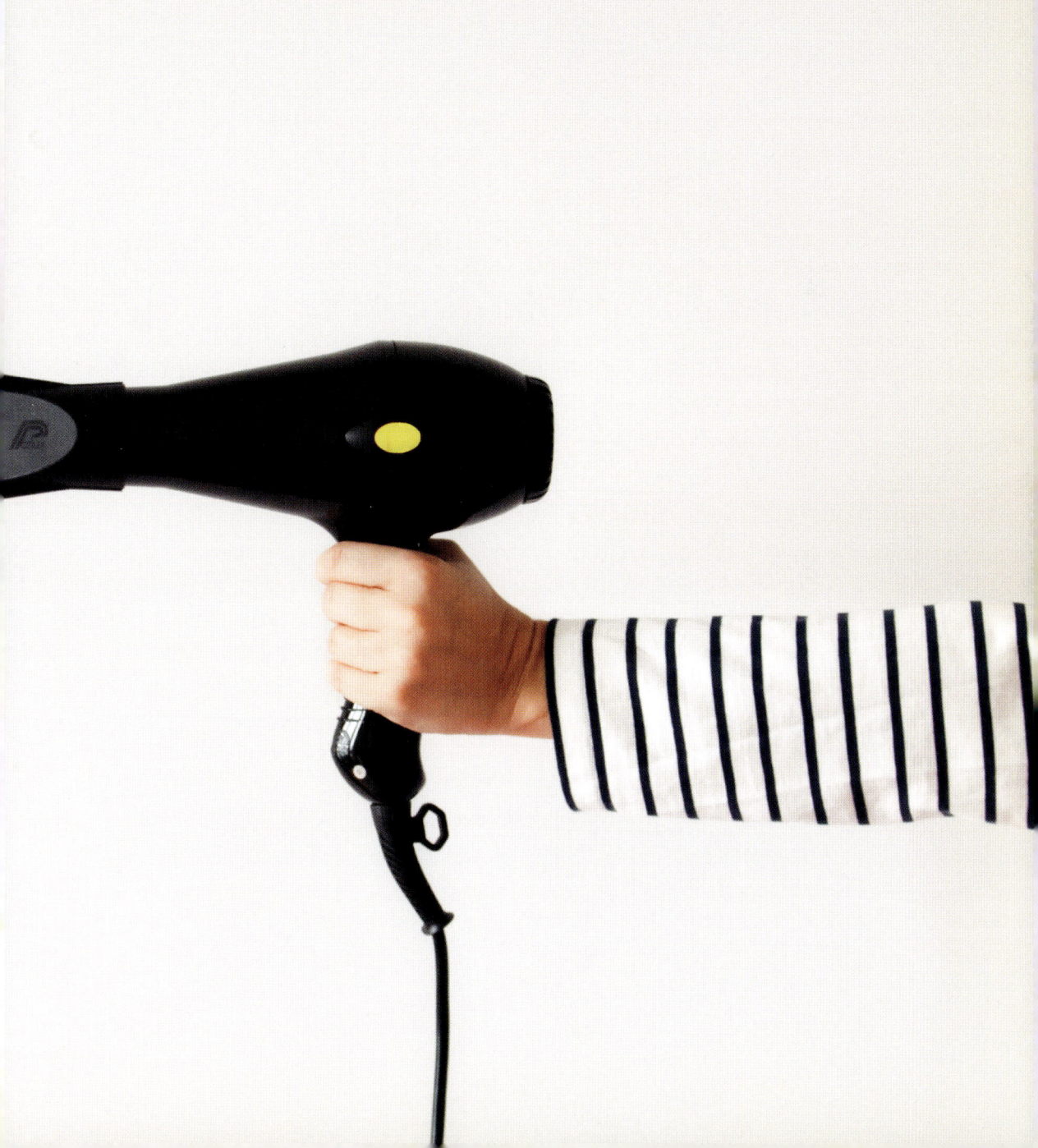

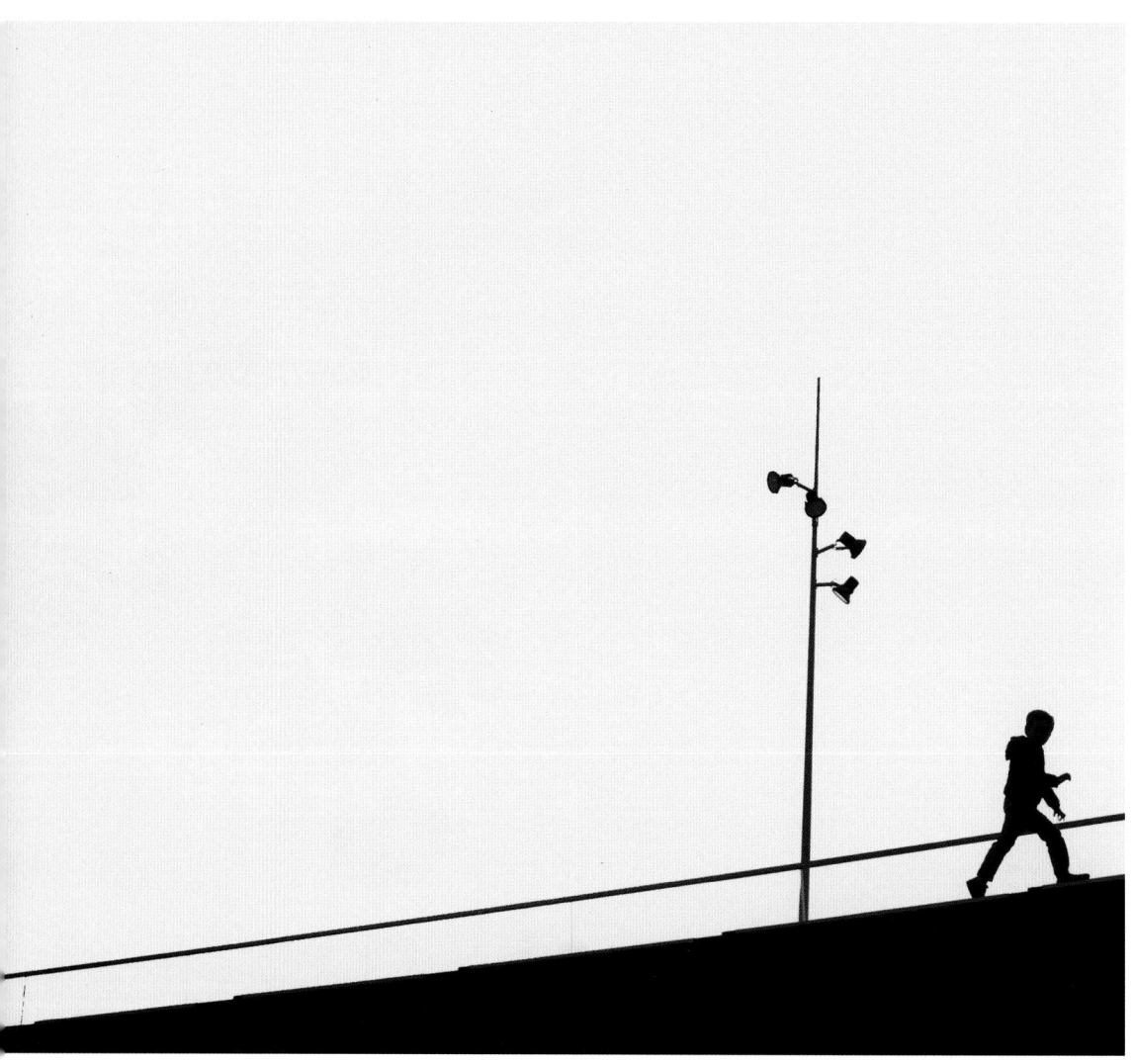

Steps away from reality

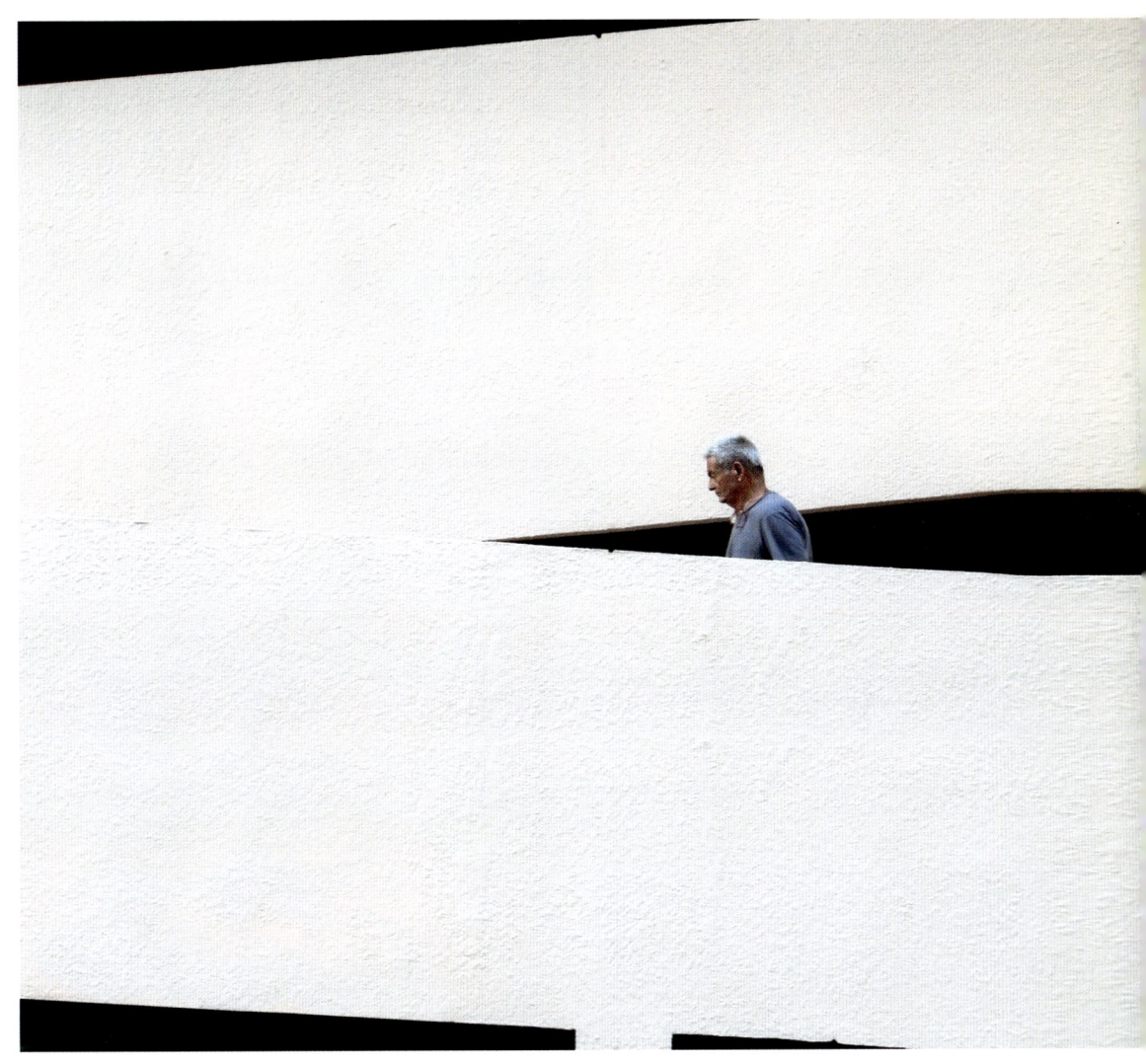

Small people, big zebras

Imagine

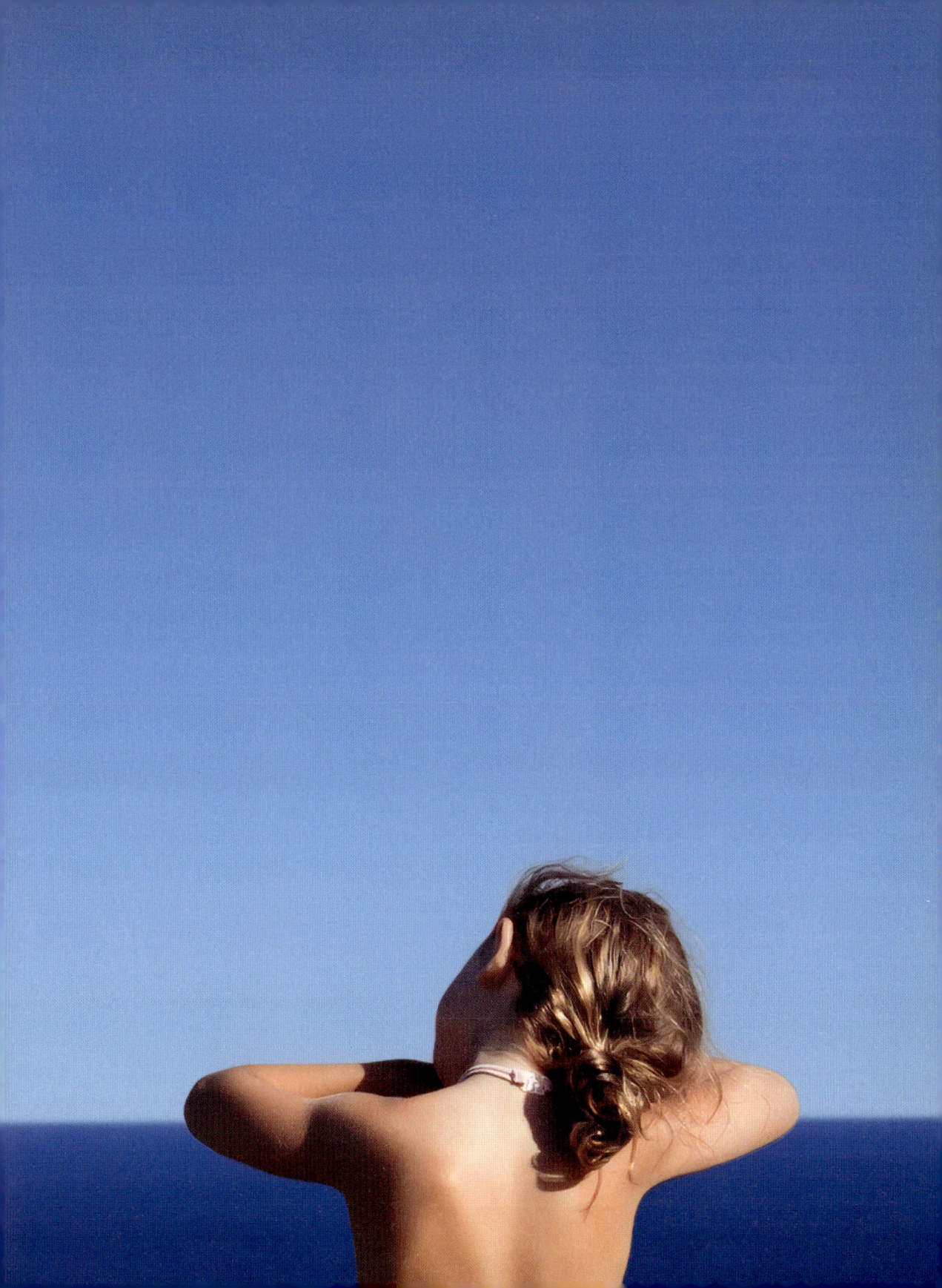

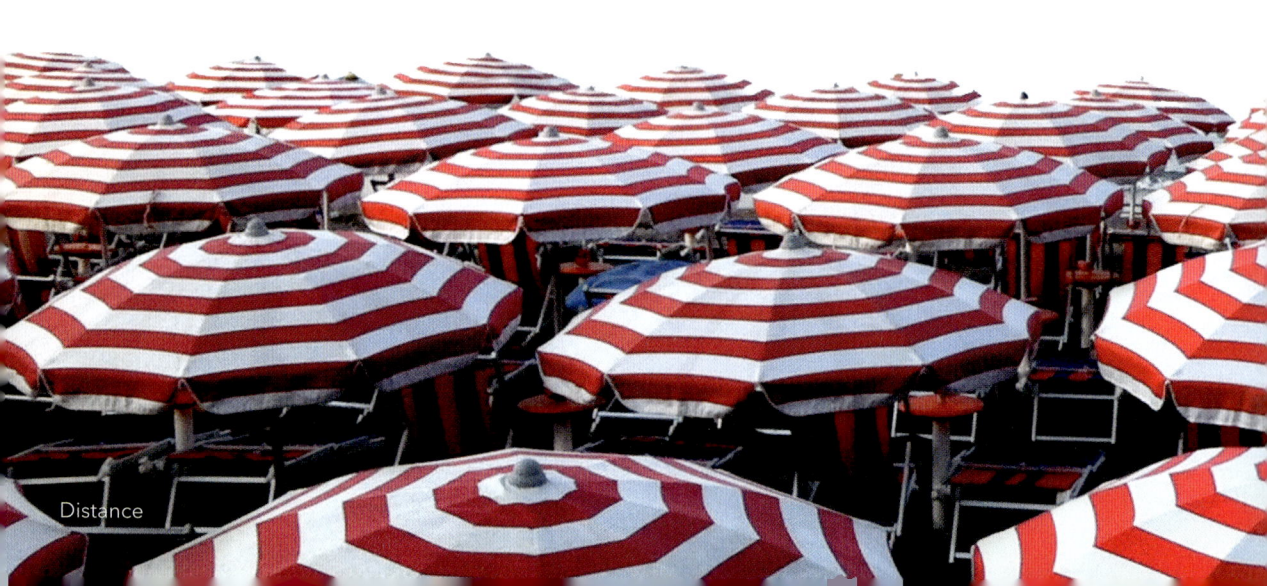

Distance

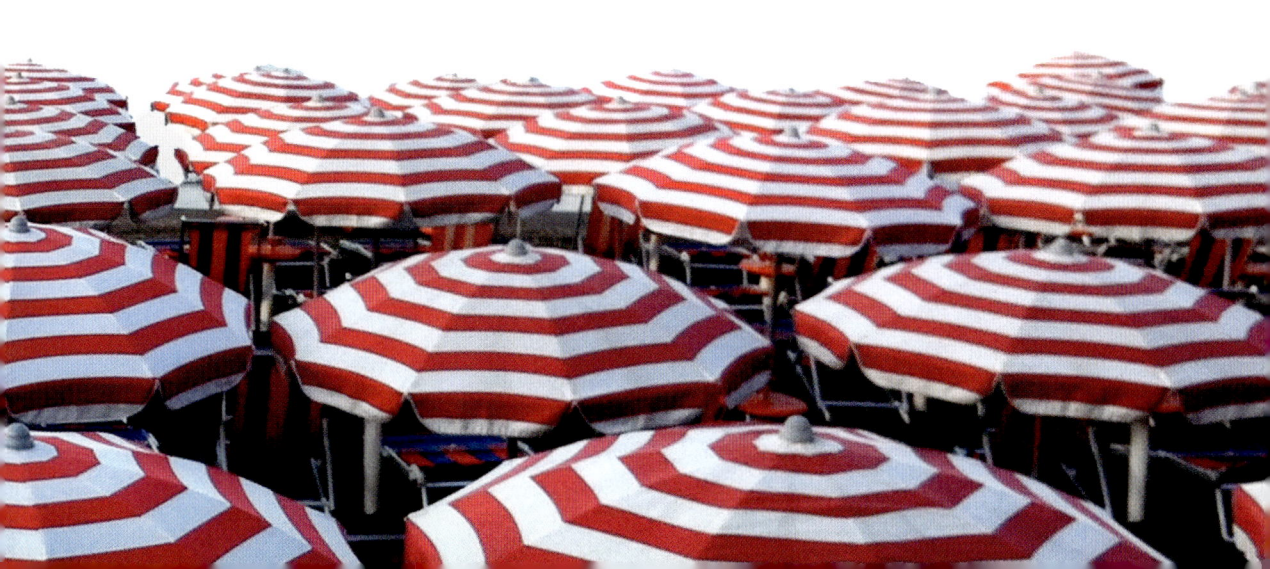

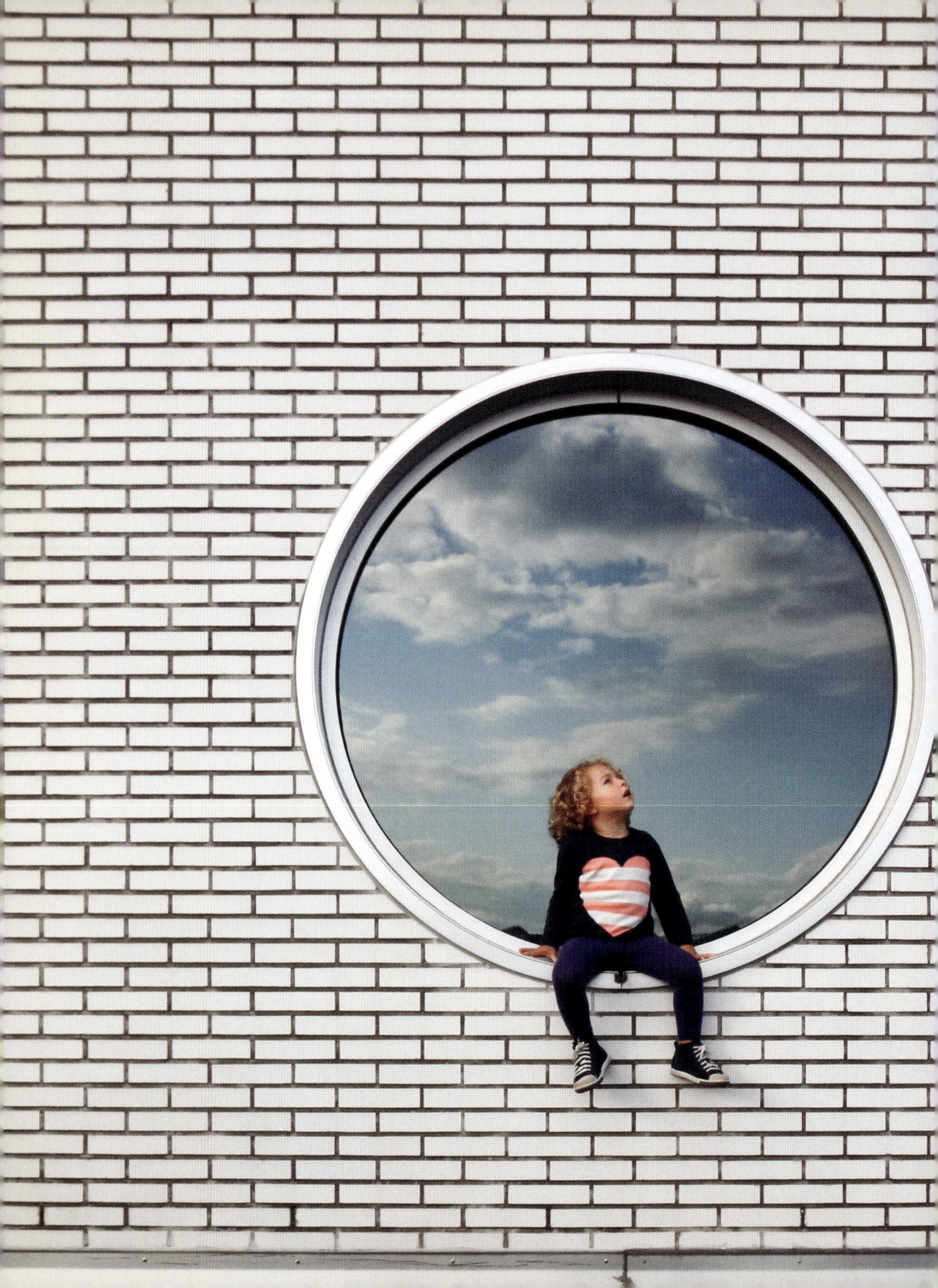

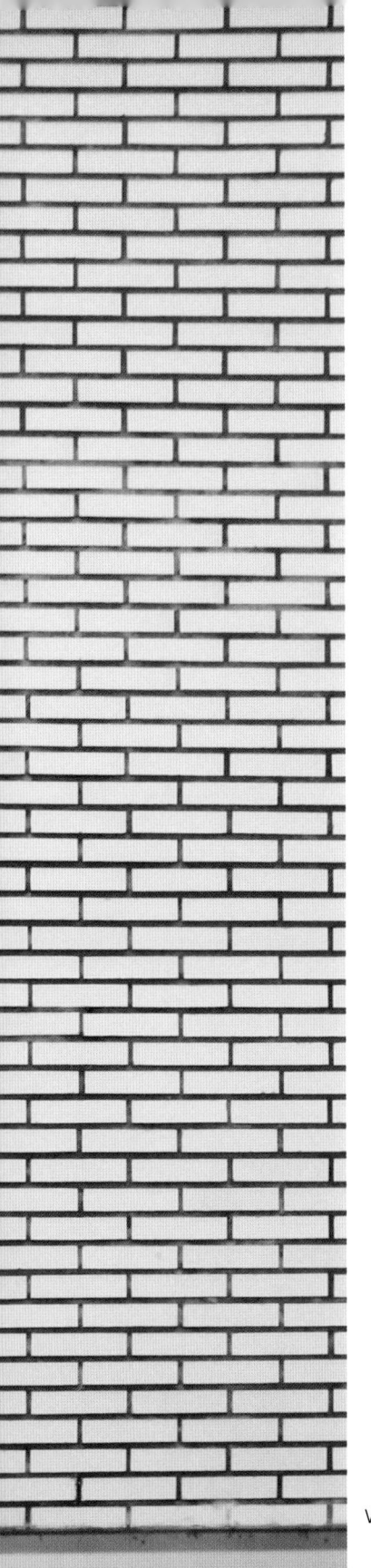

Watching machine

Find the panda

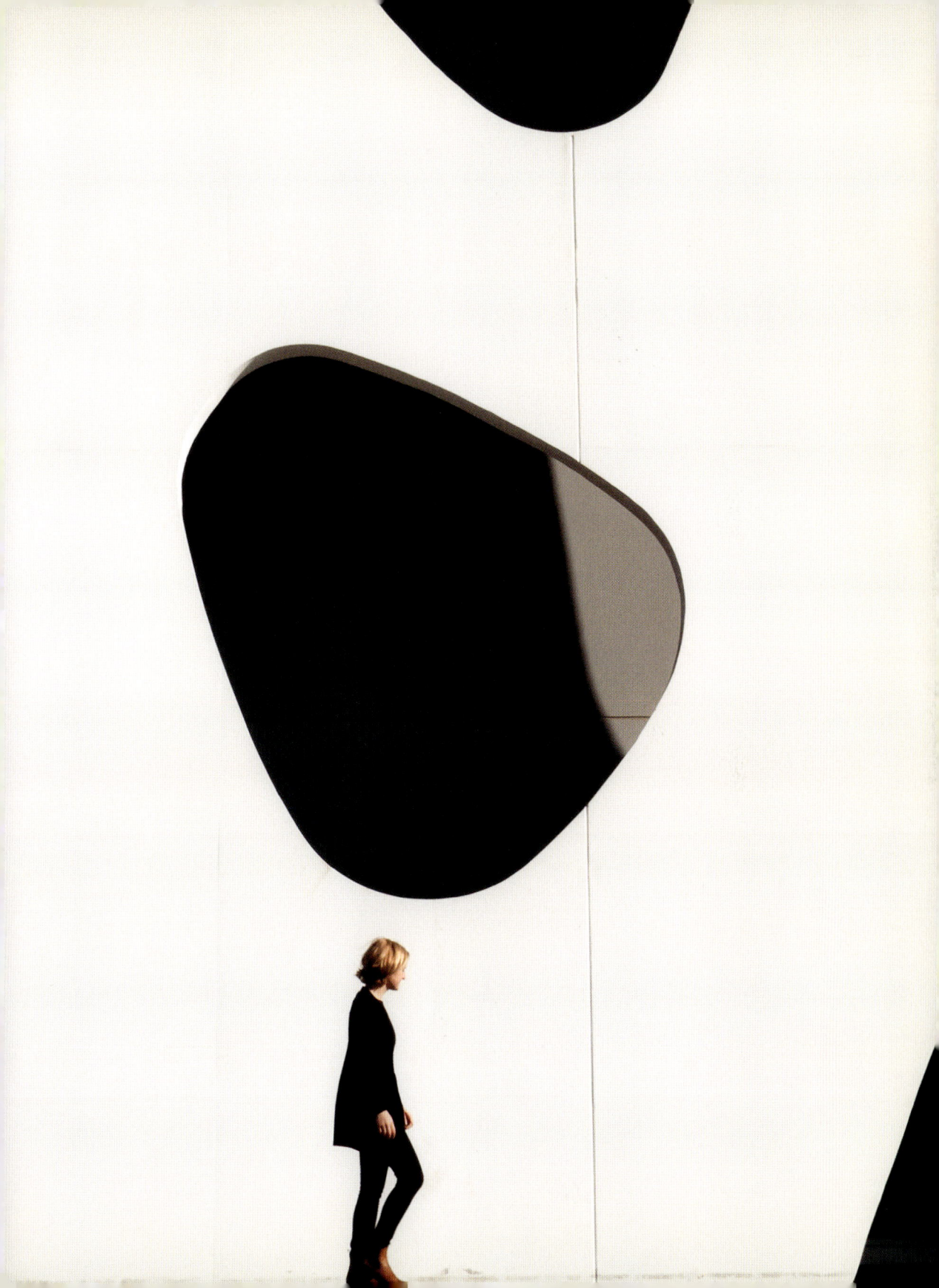

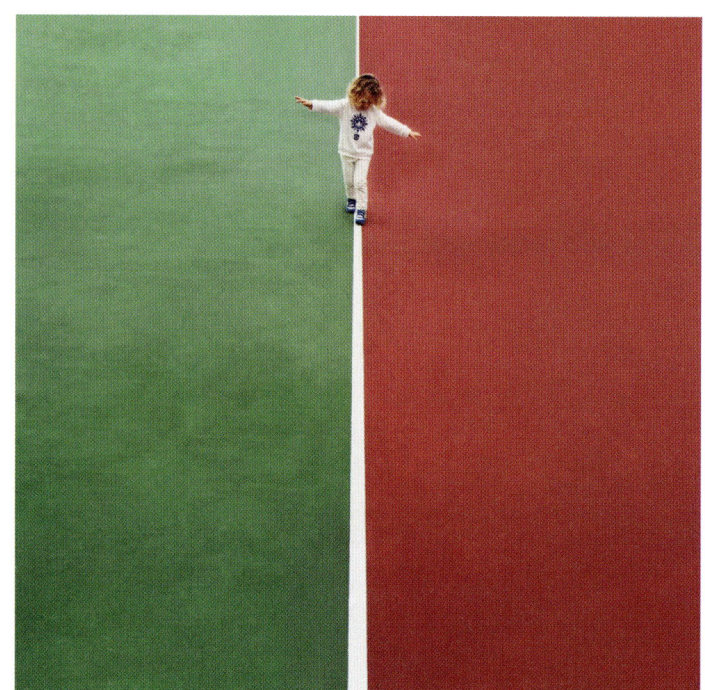

Italy

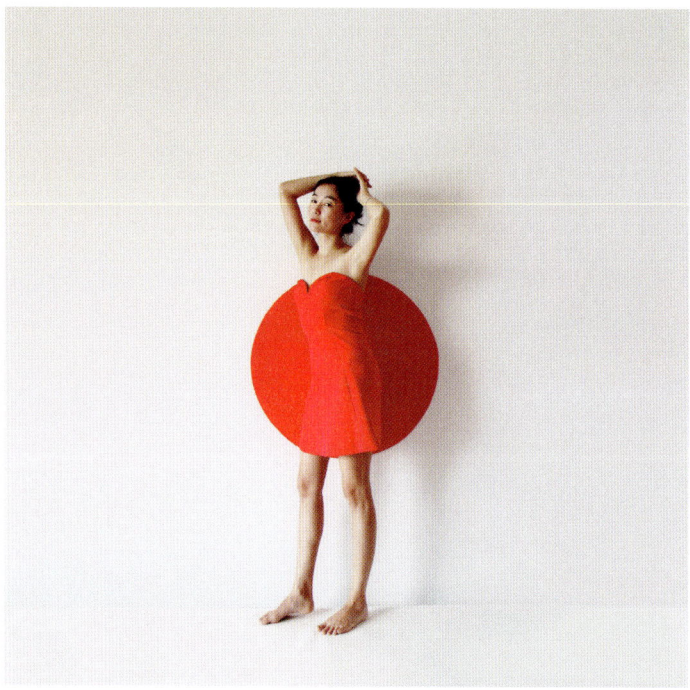

Japan

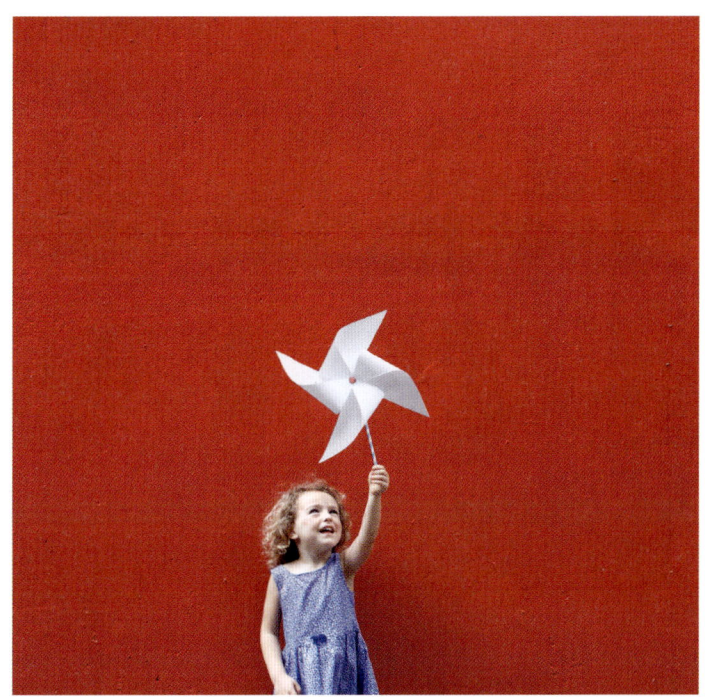

Hong Kong

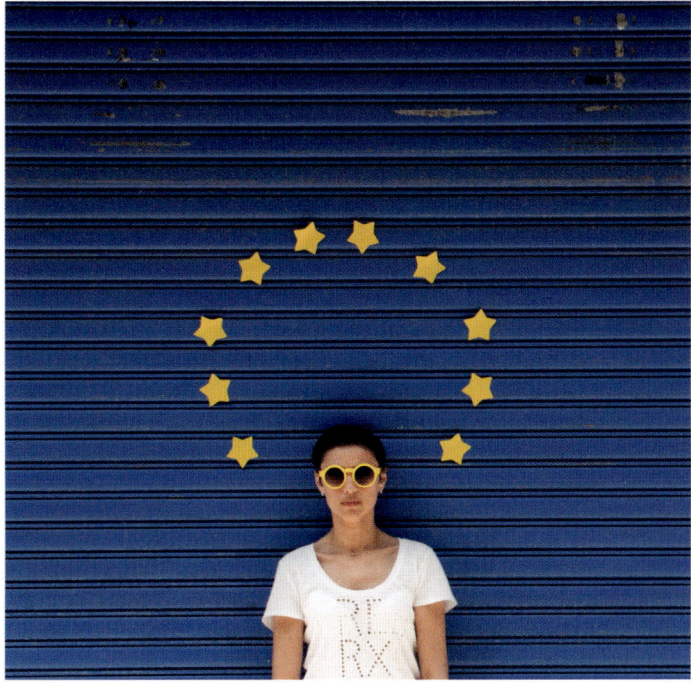

Europe

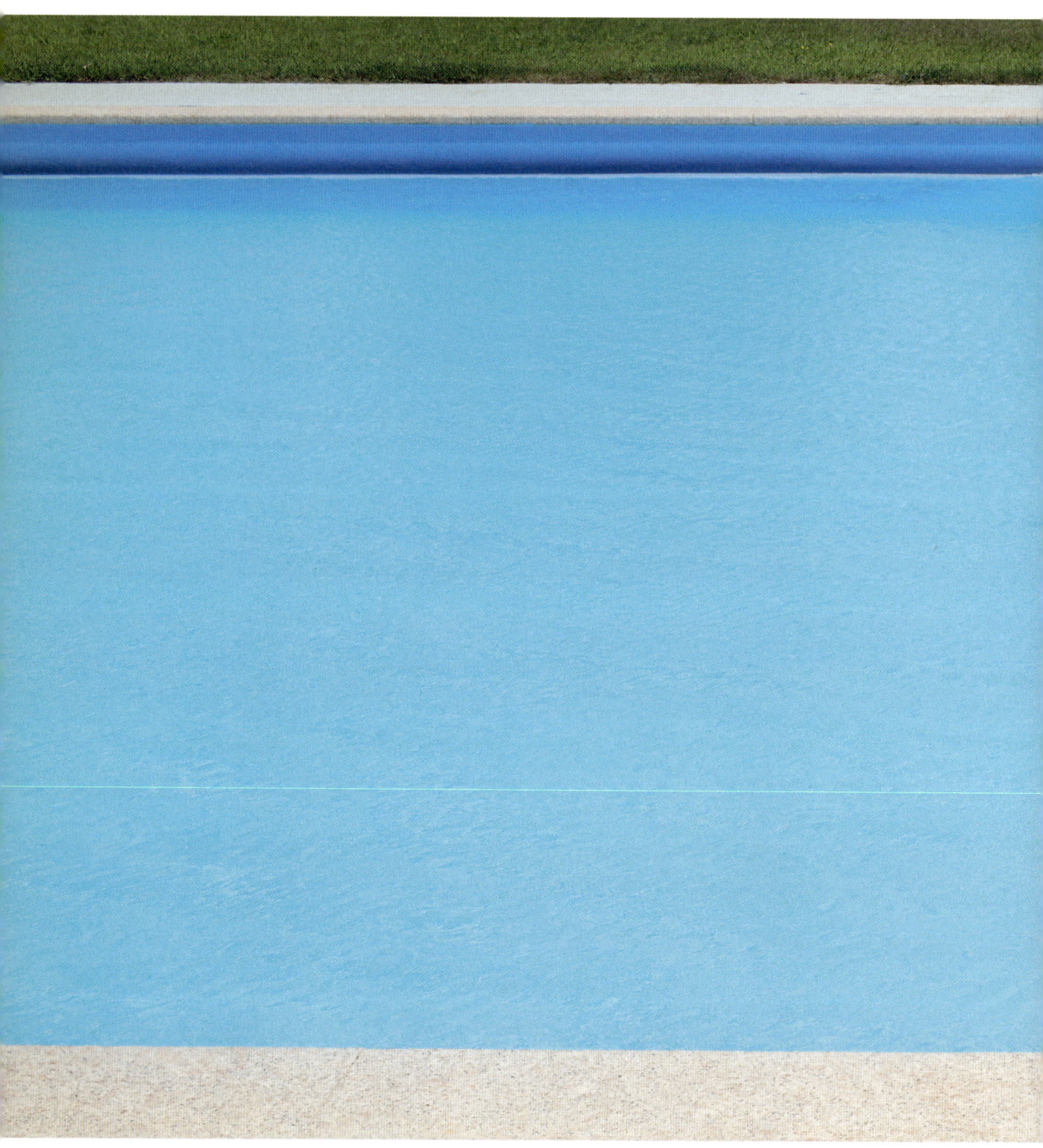

Until further notice

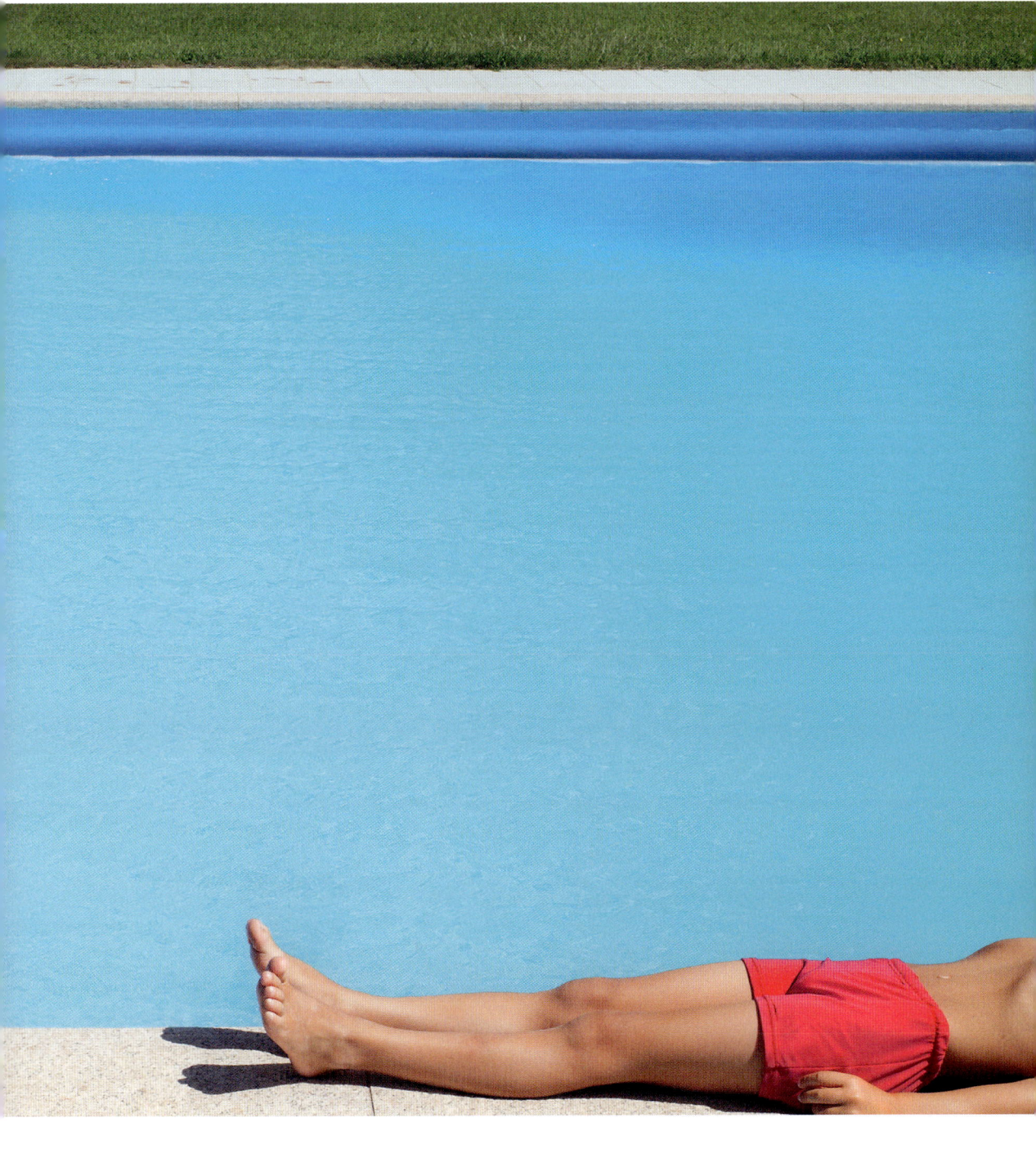

This love is silent

Width by height

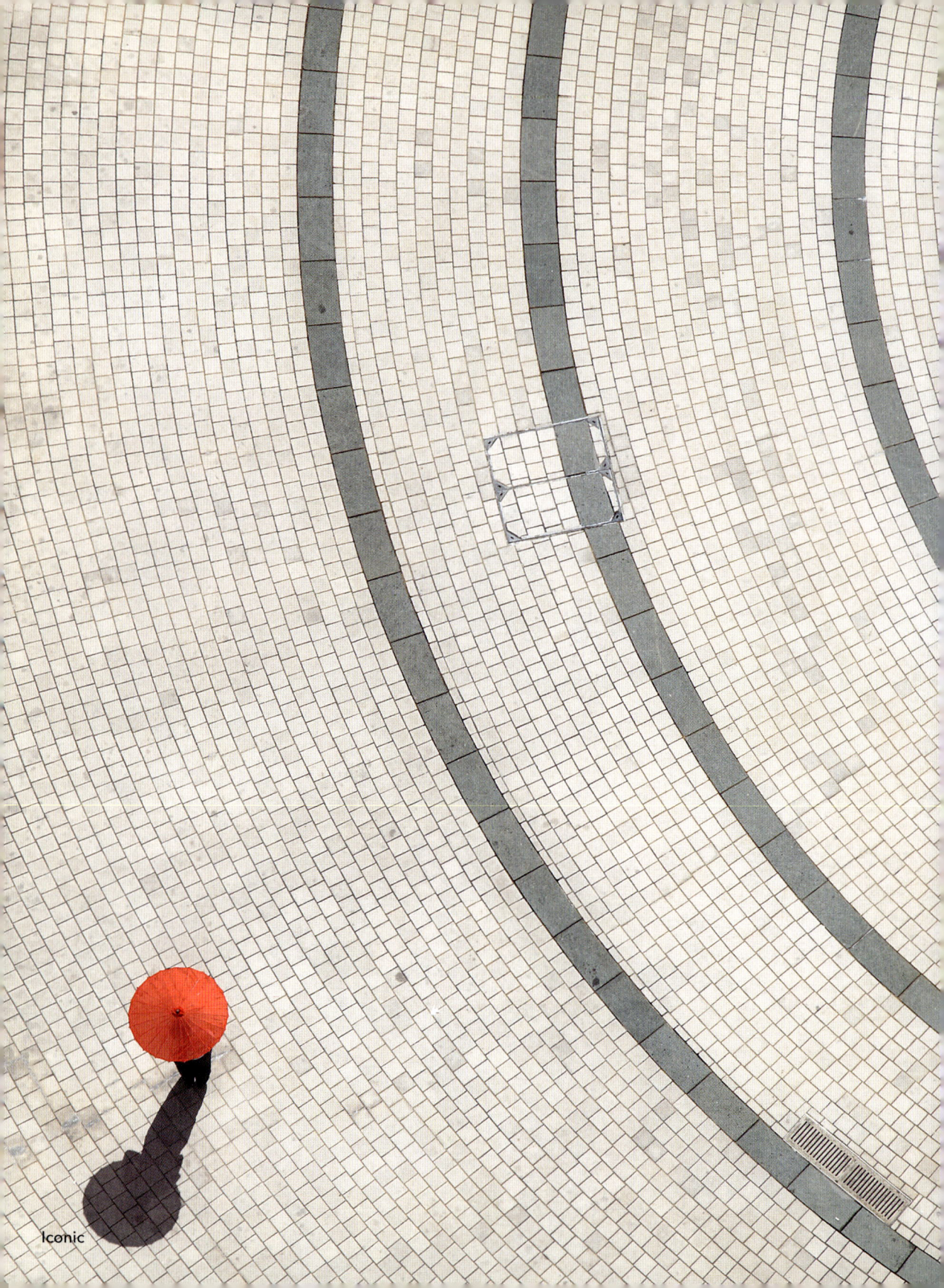

Iconic

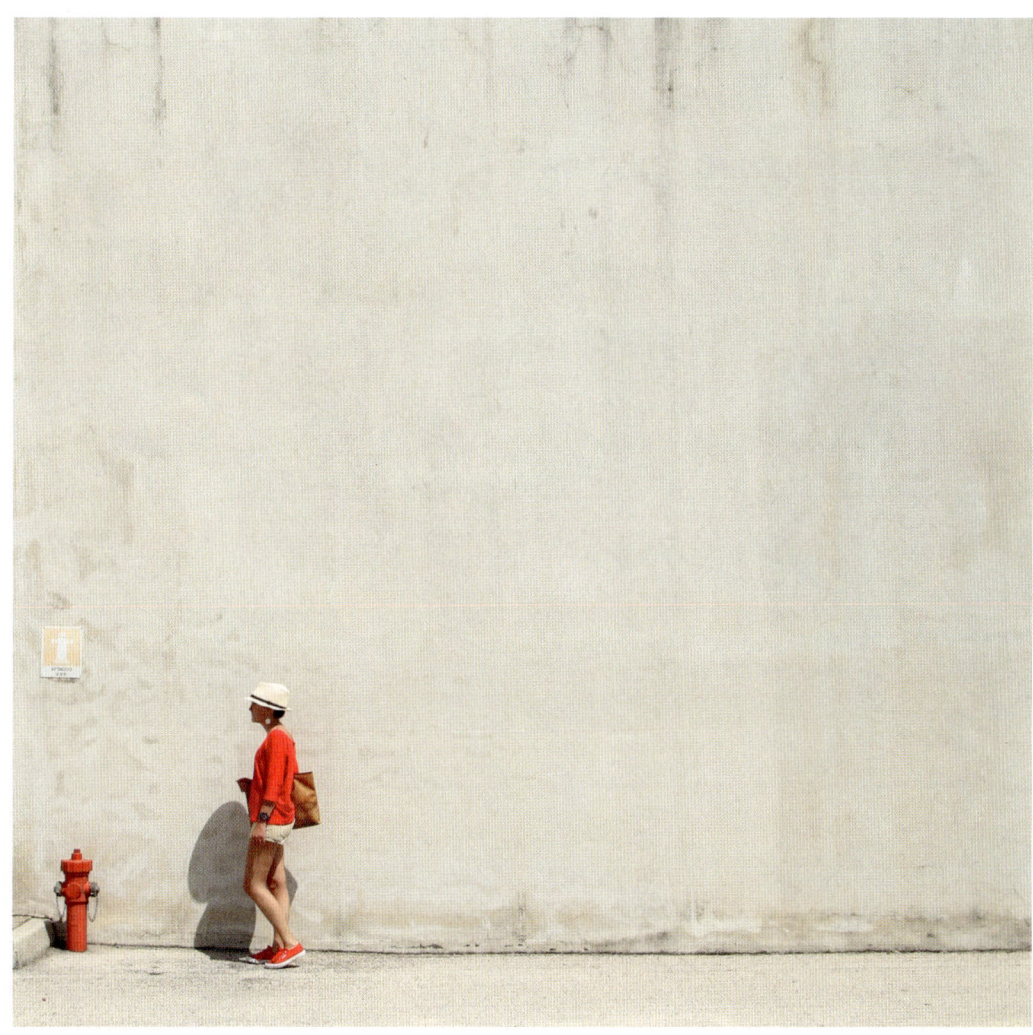

InspiRED

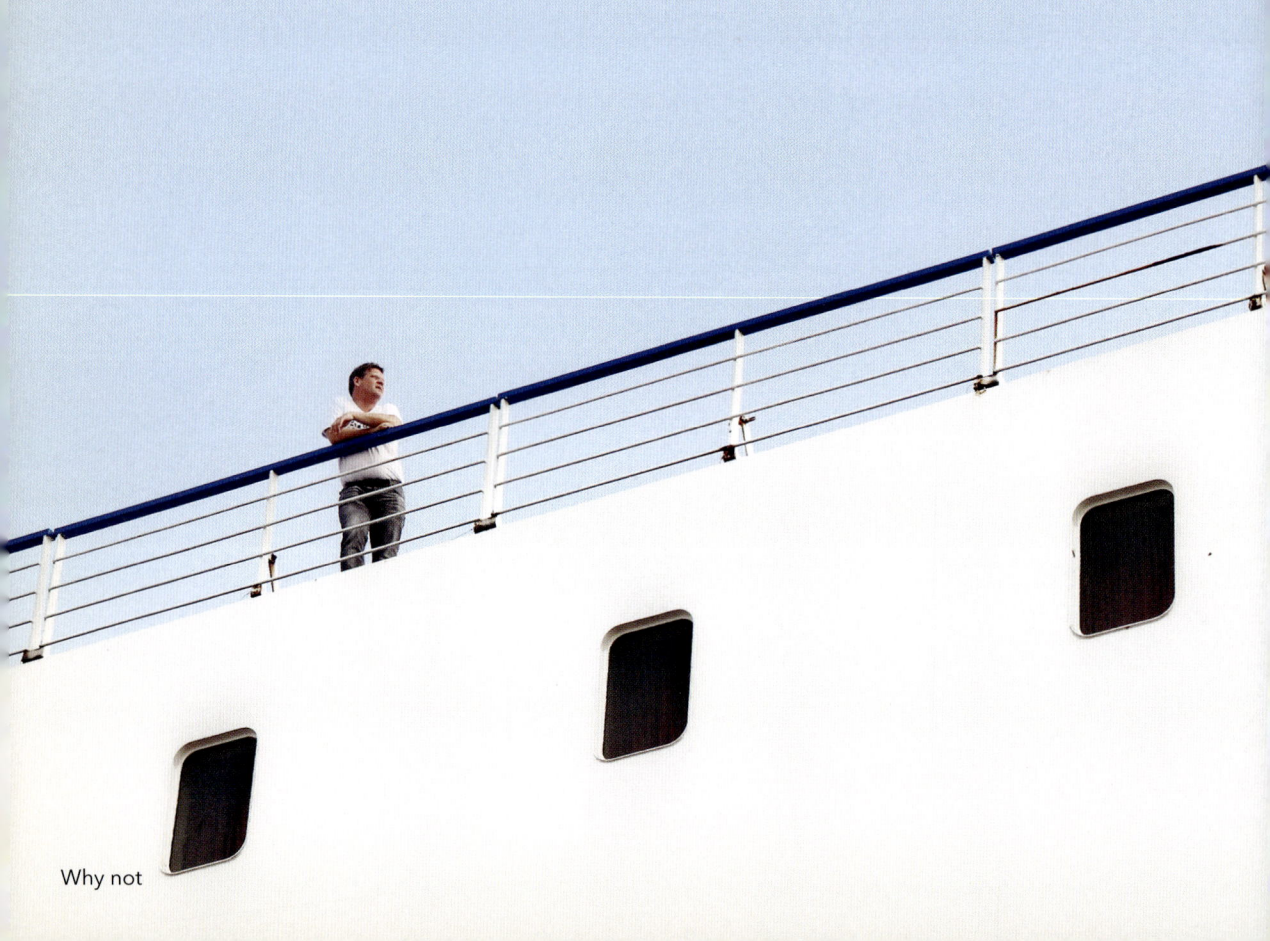

Why not

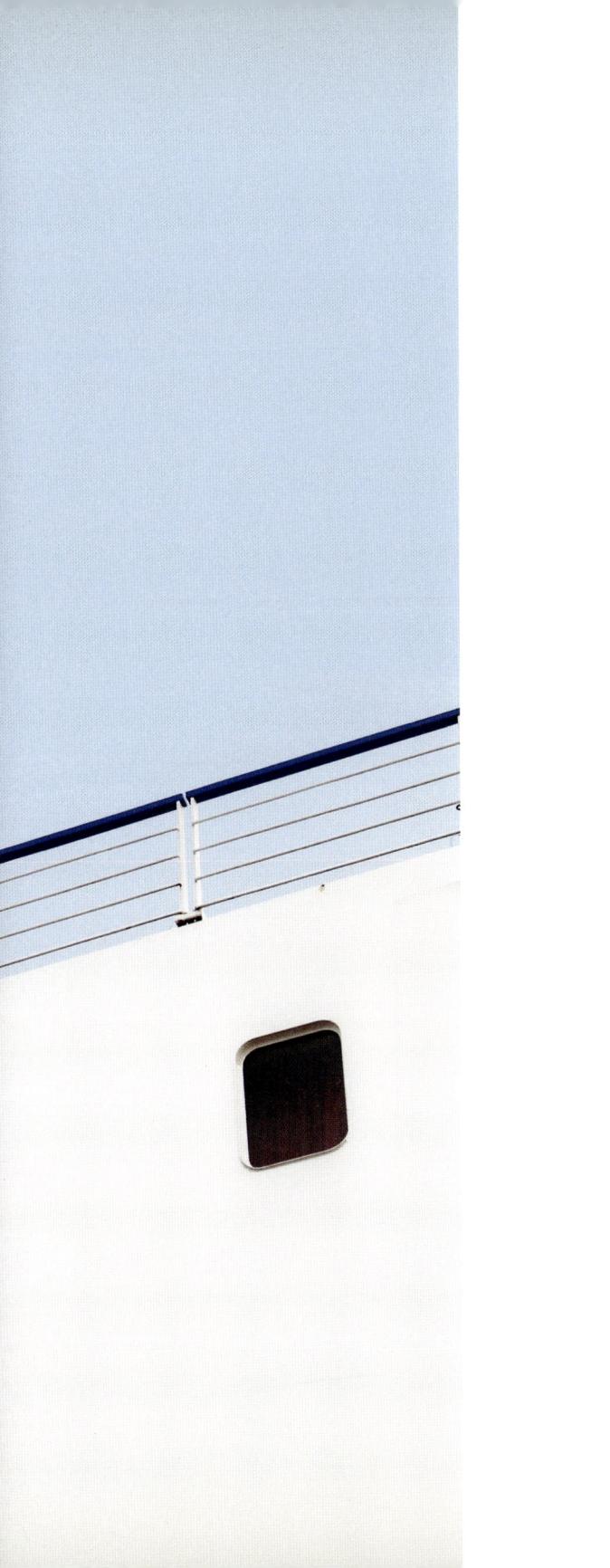

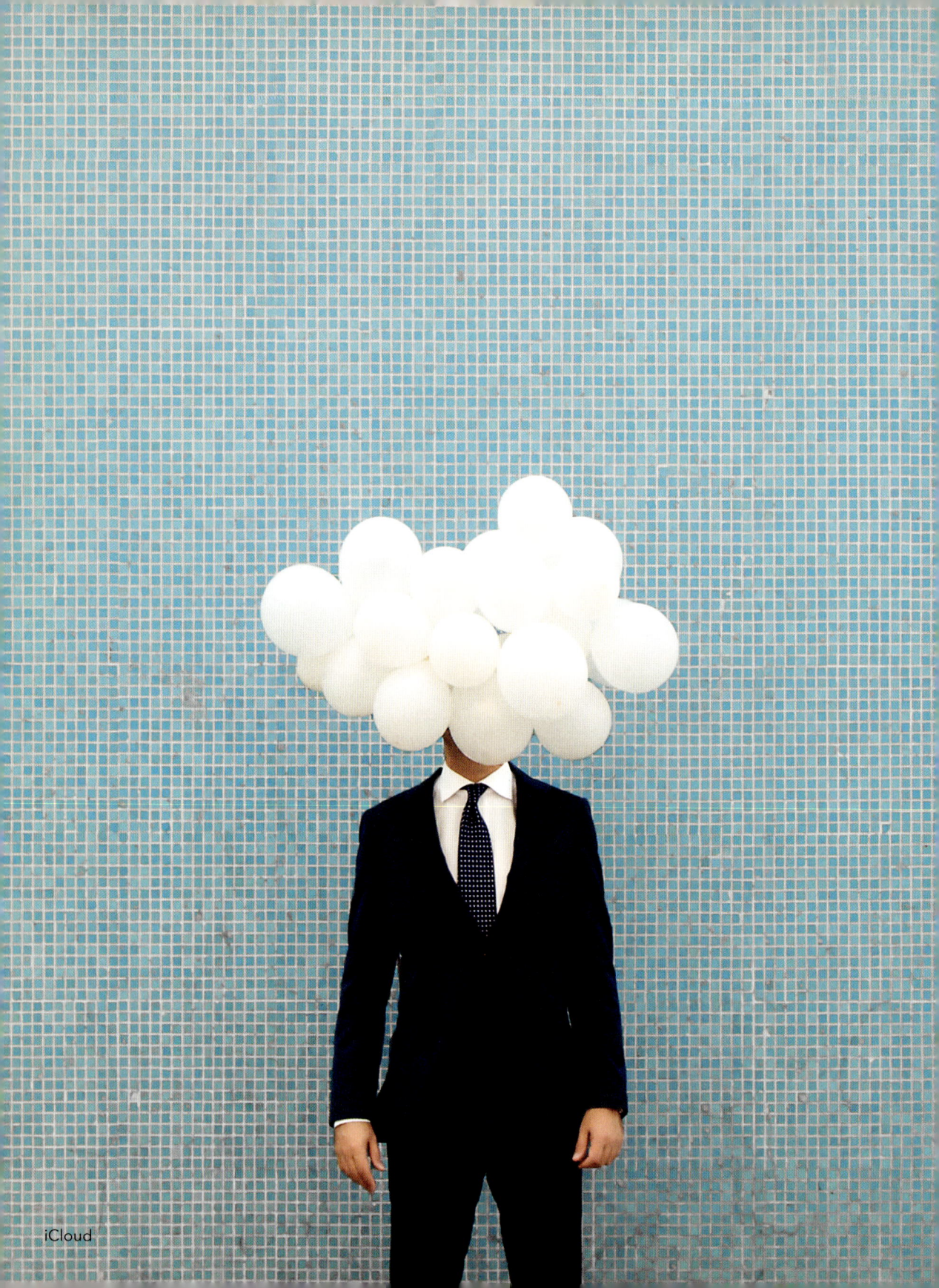

iCloud

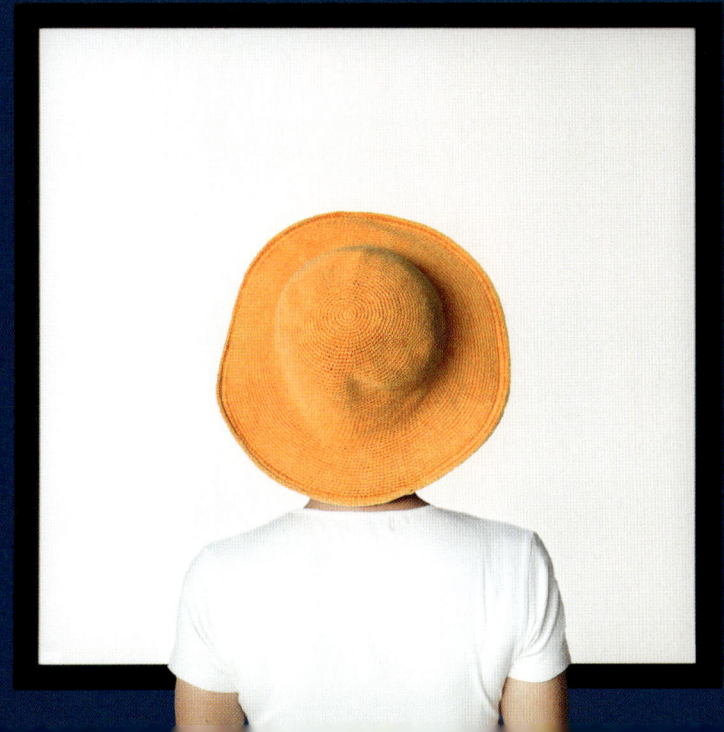

Sunny side up

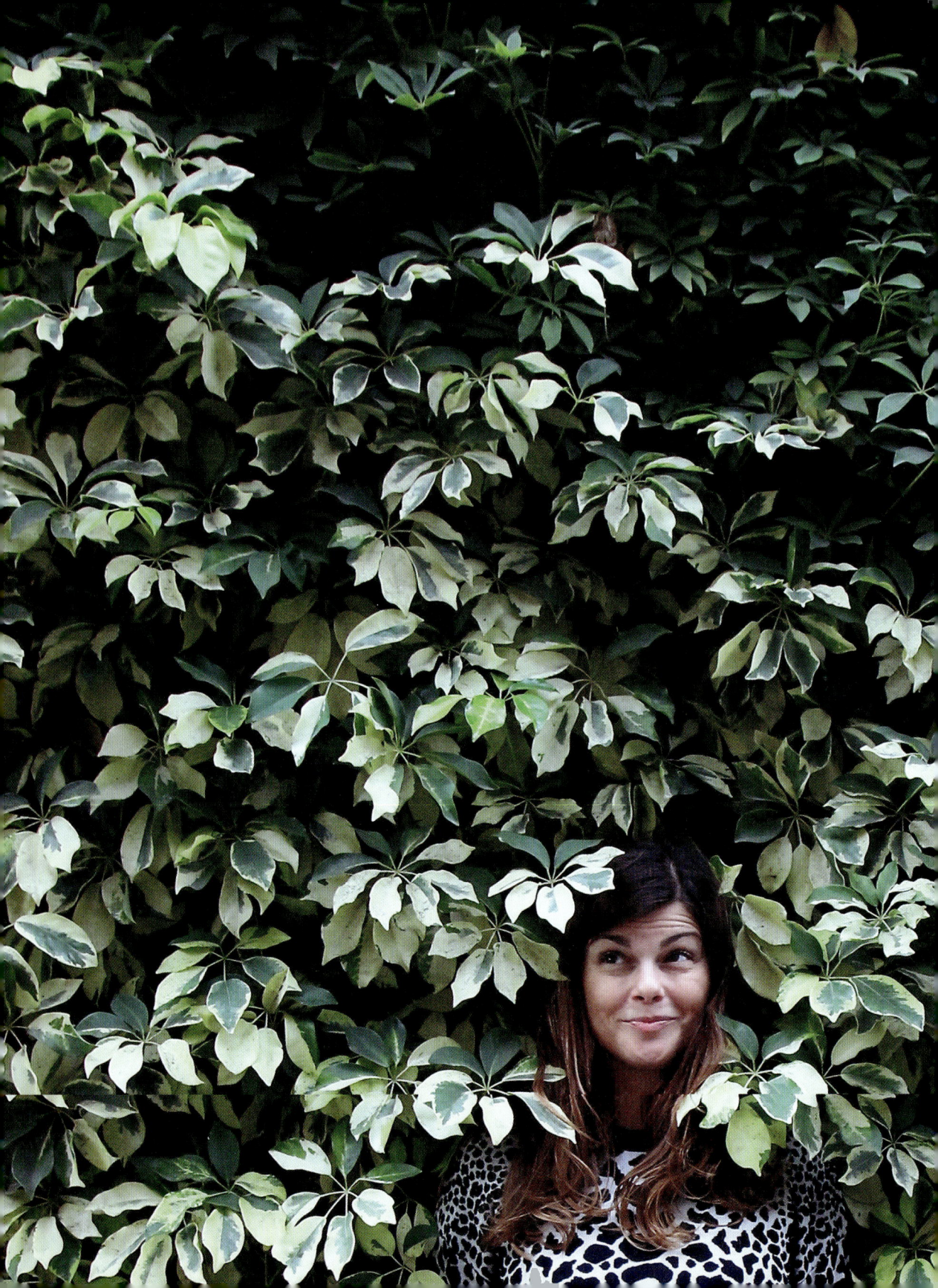

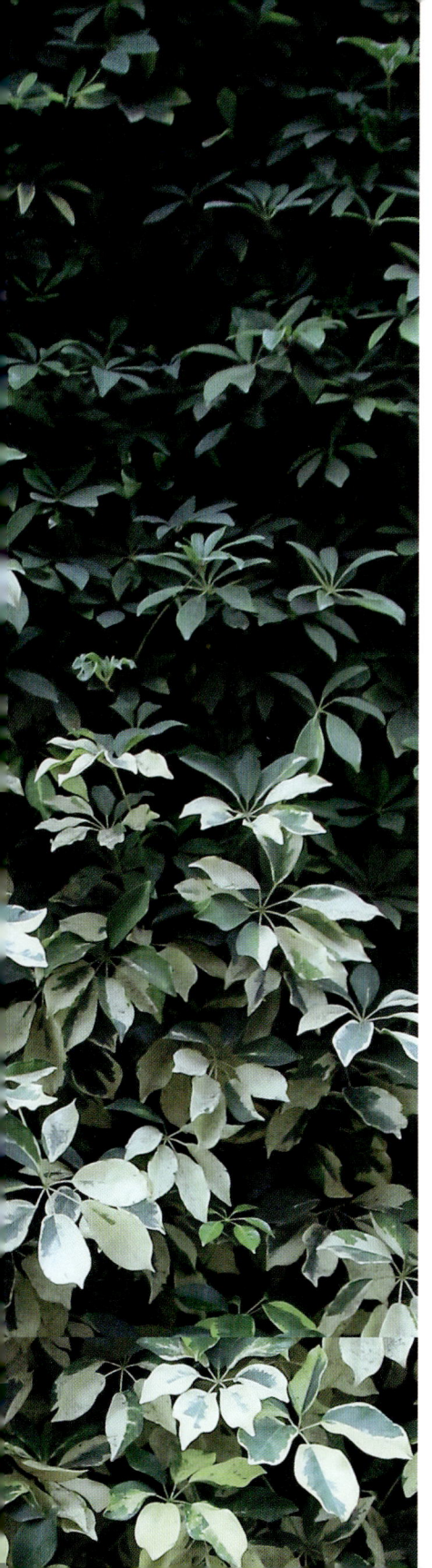

I can explain

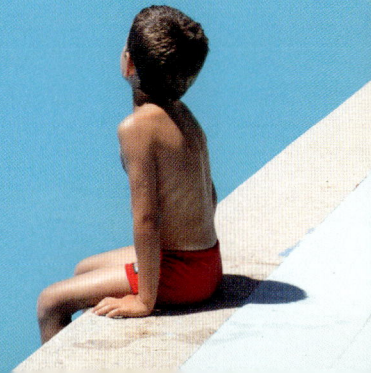

Little

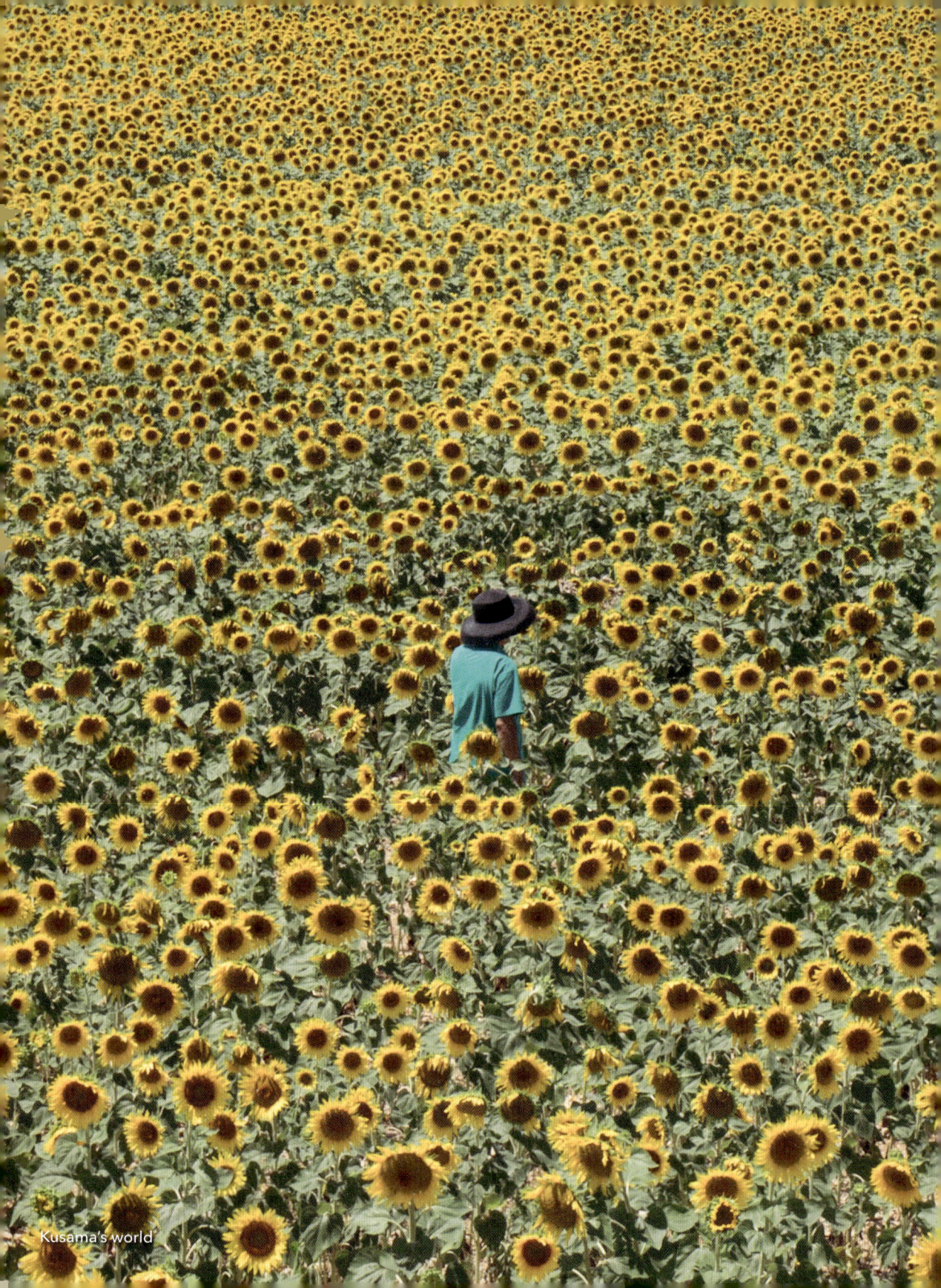

Kusama's world

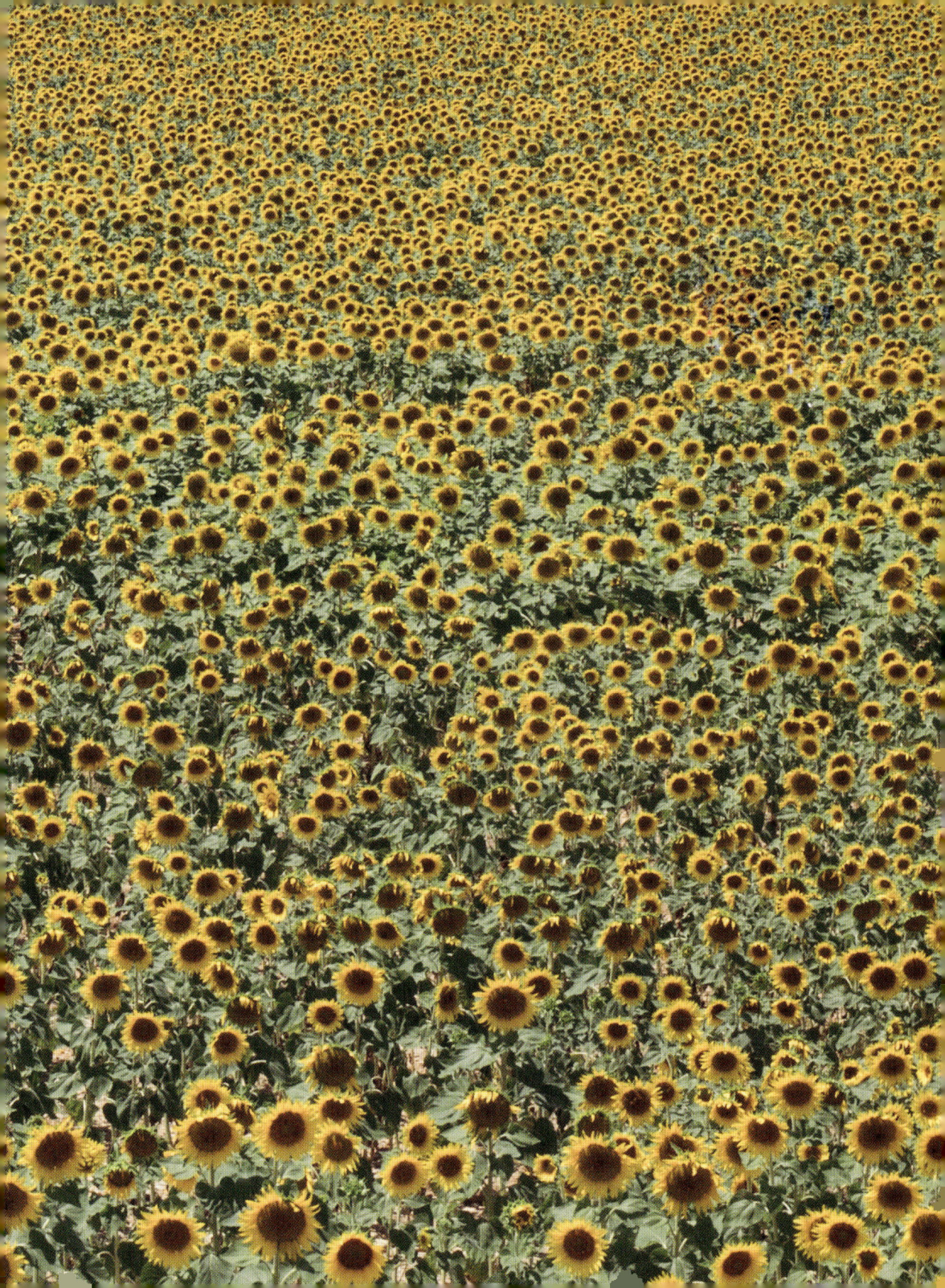

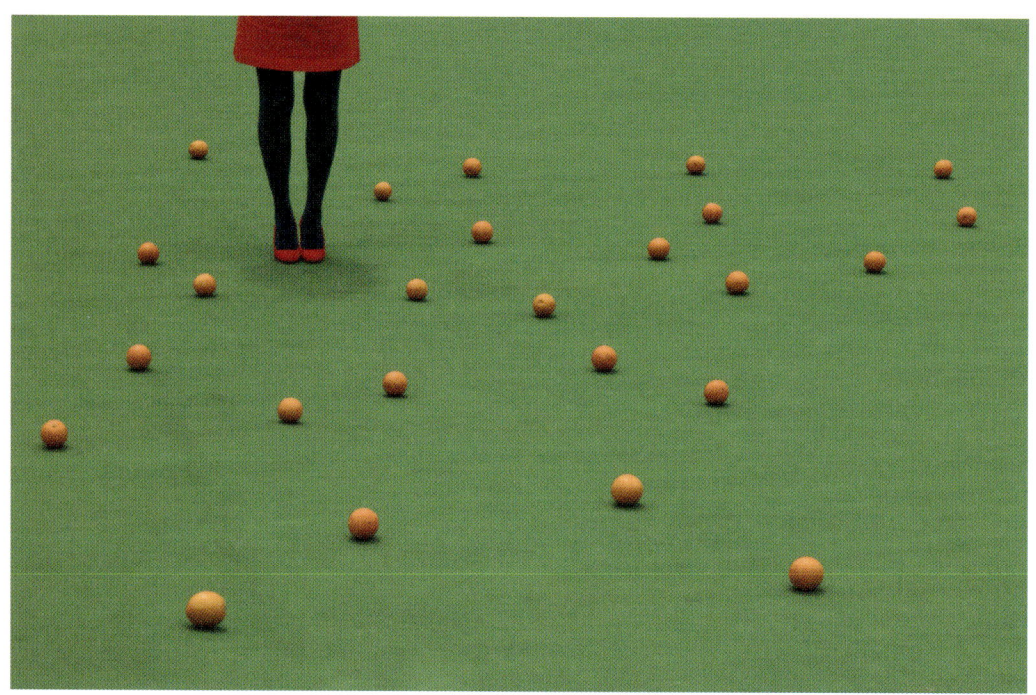

Keep quiet

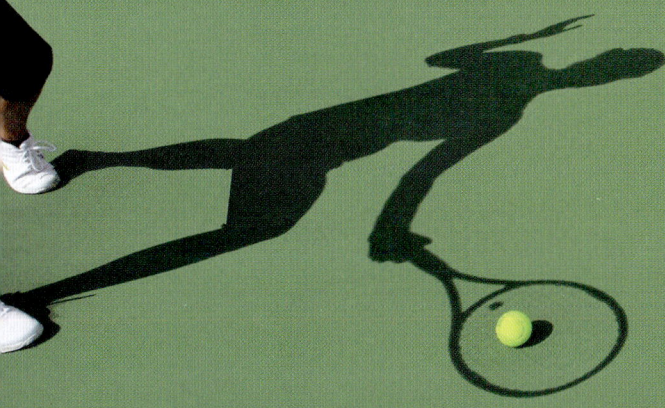

Hit and miss

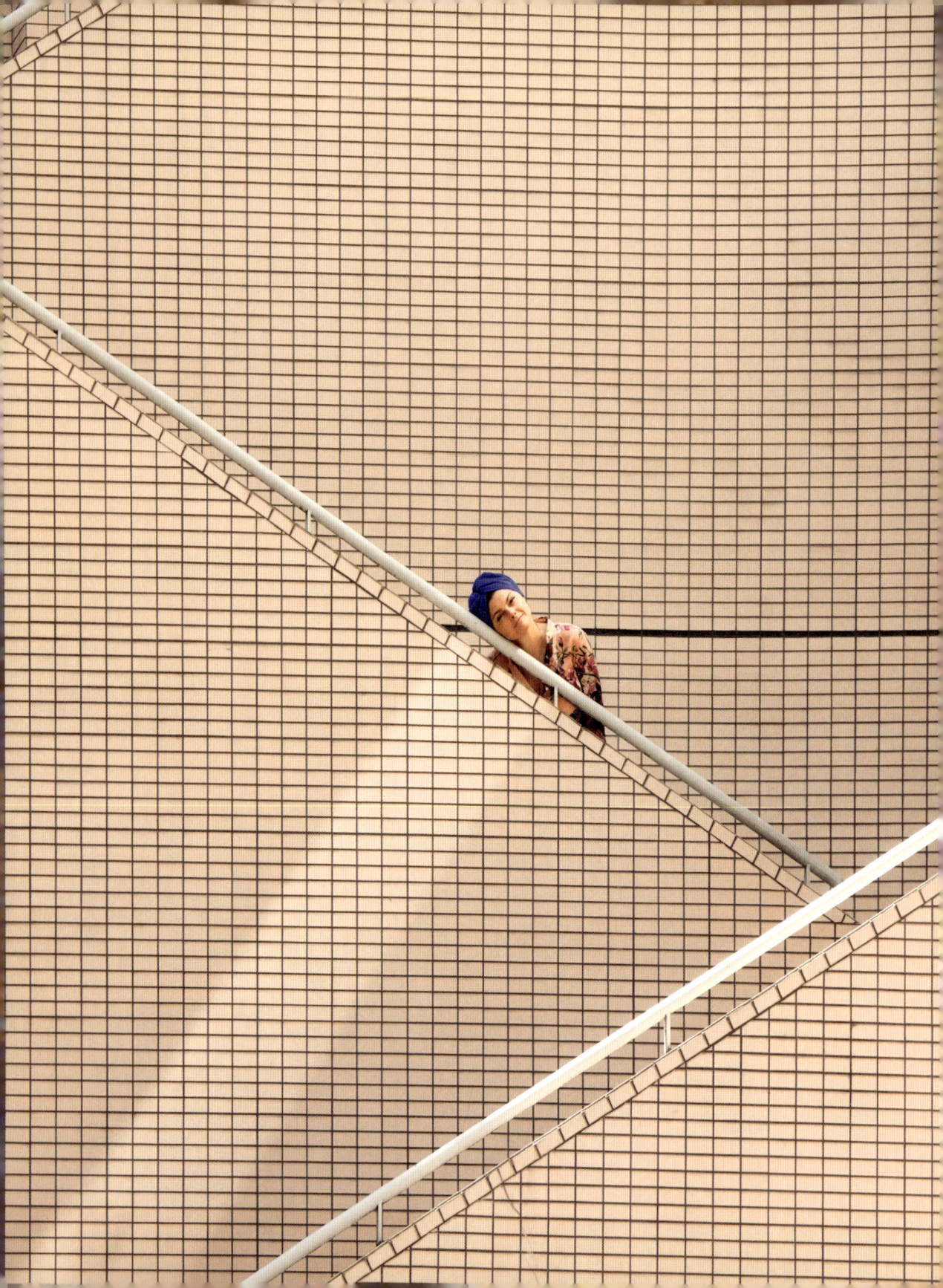

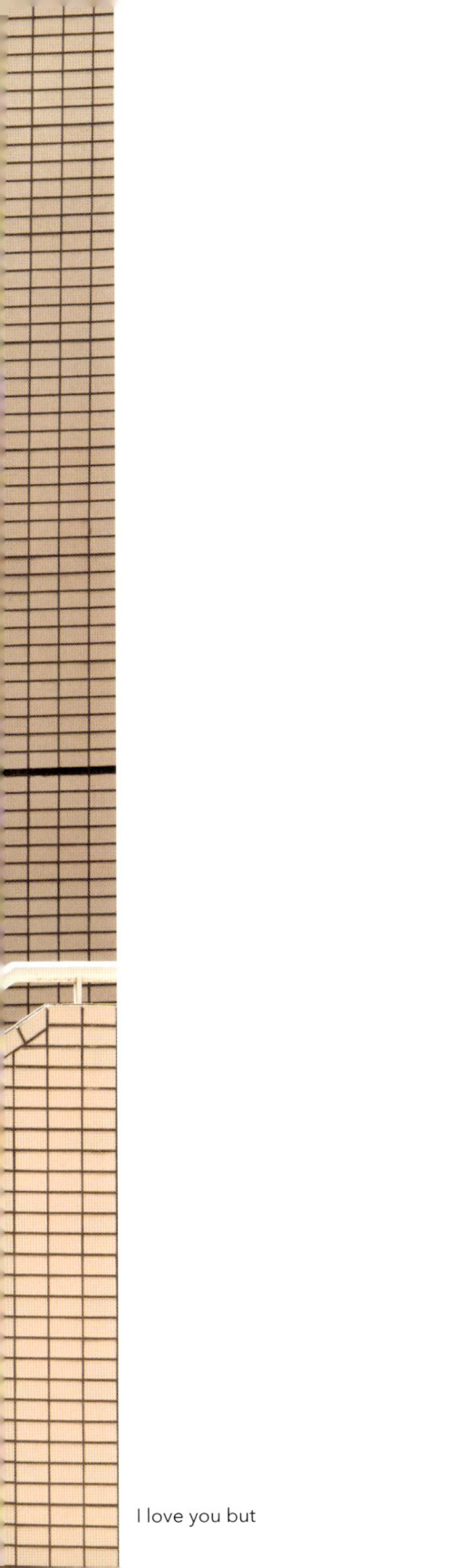

I love you but

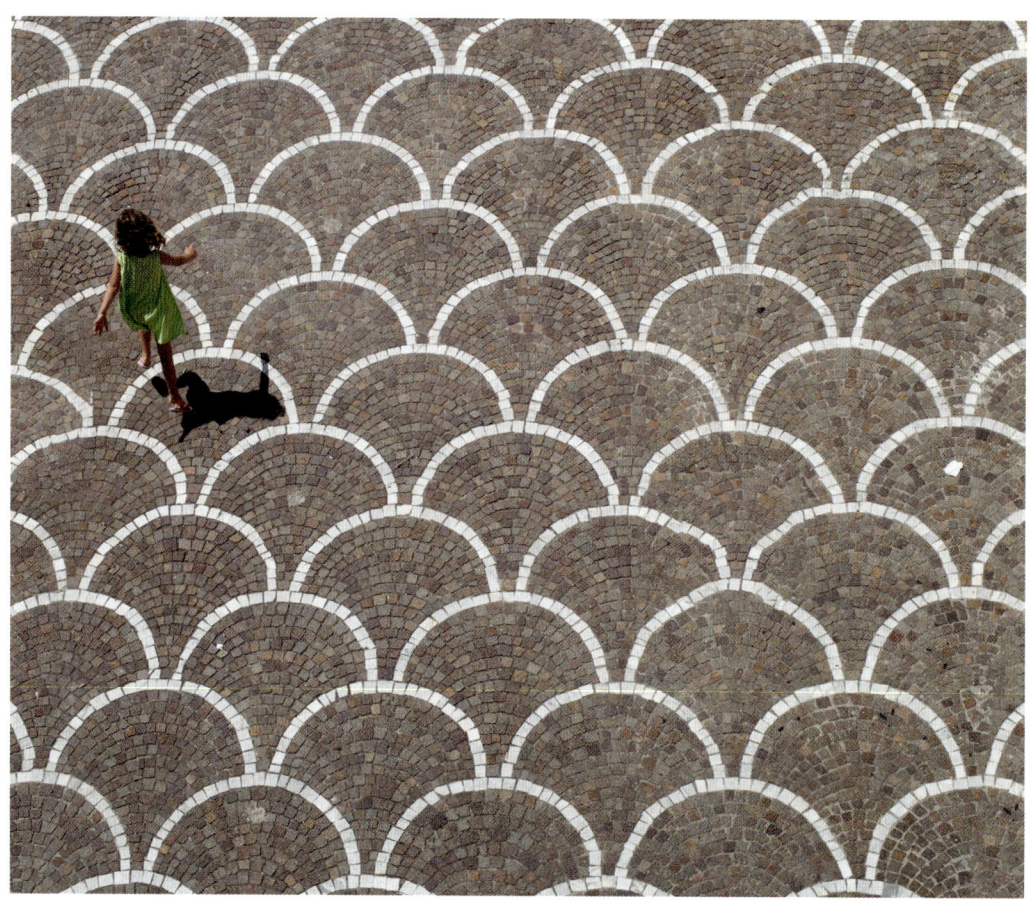

Mom, did you know that carrots are made from pumpkins?

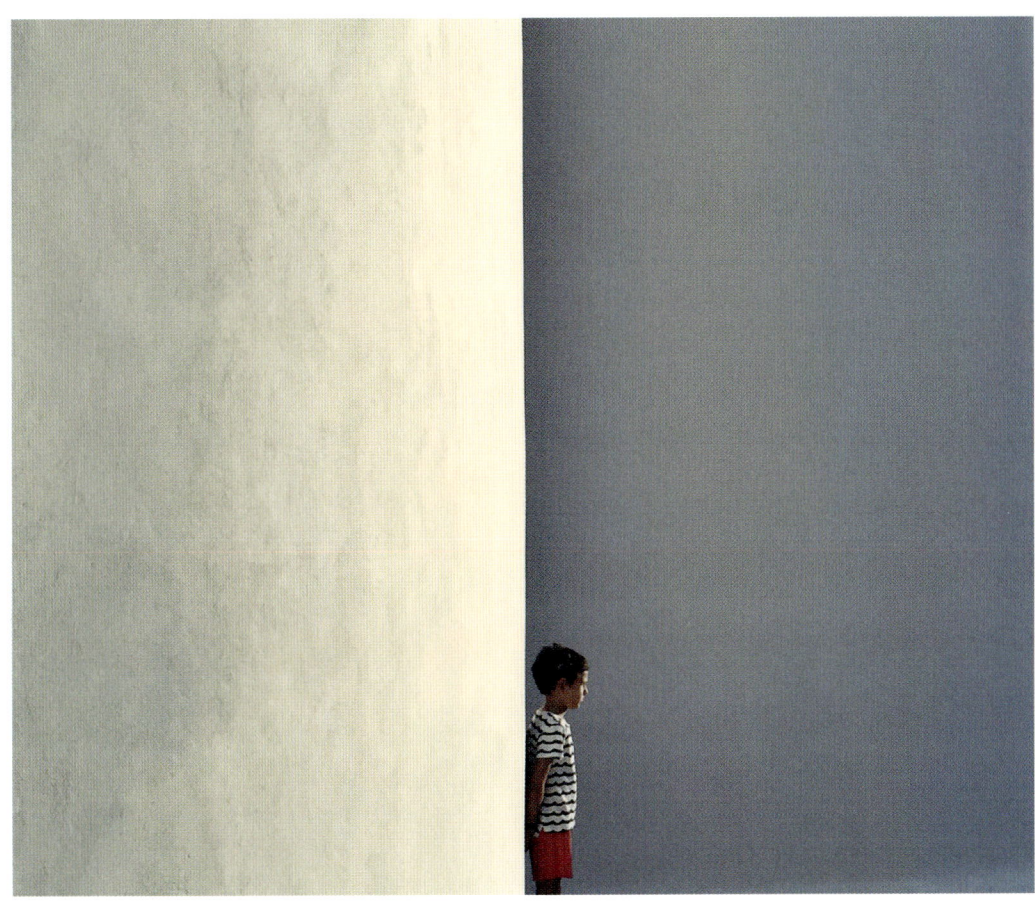

Half full

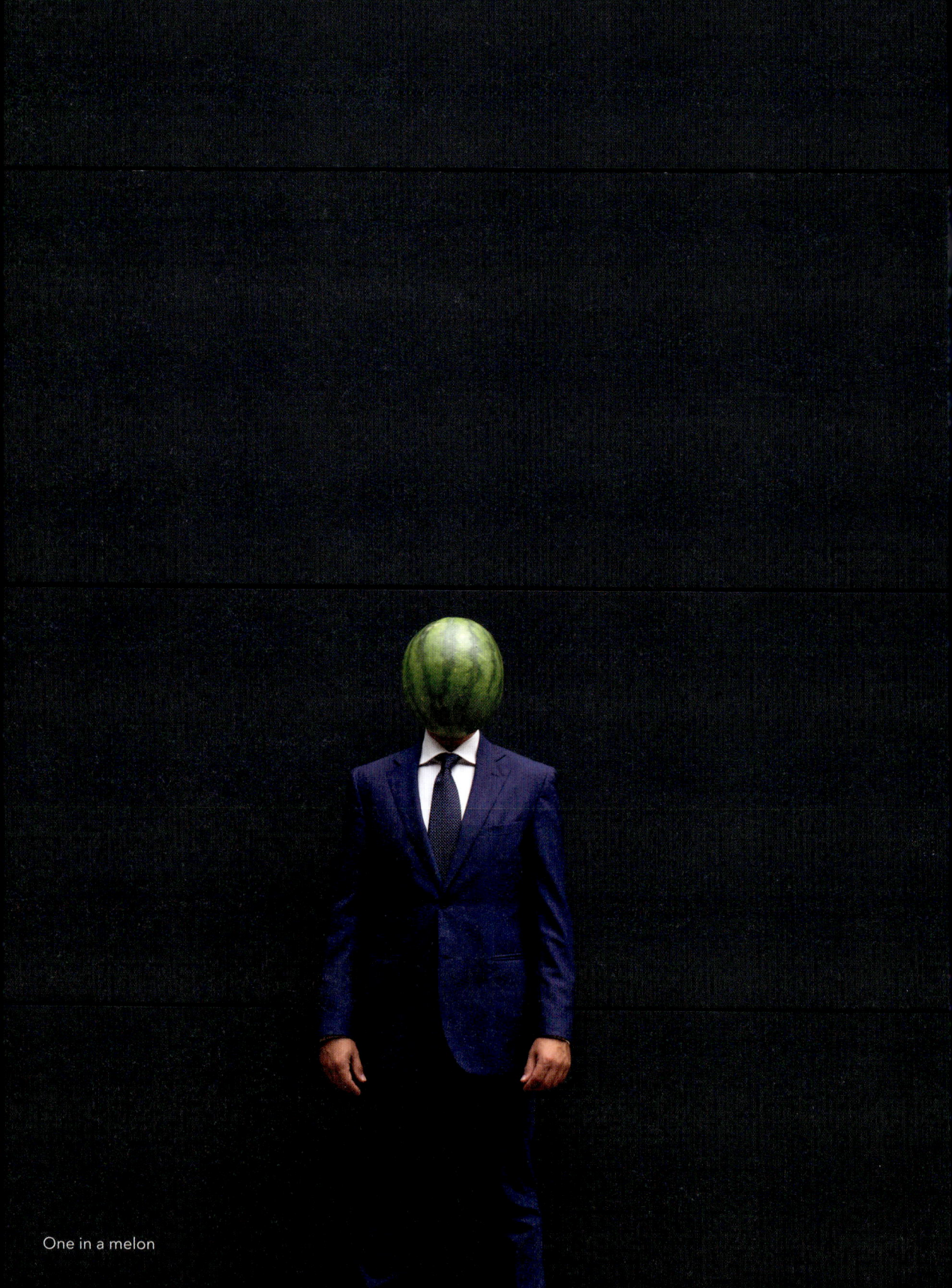

One in a melon

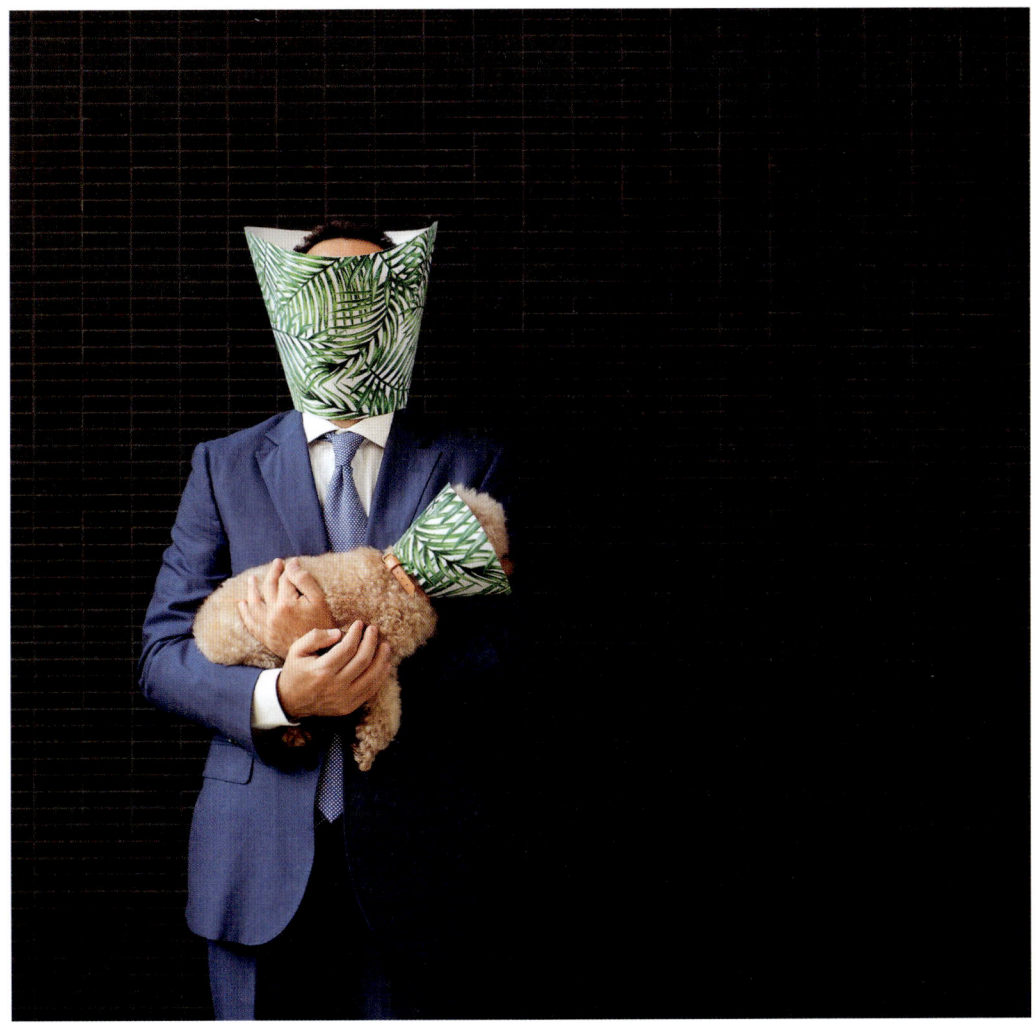

Dogman

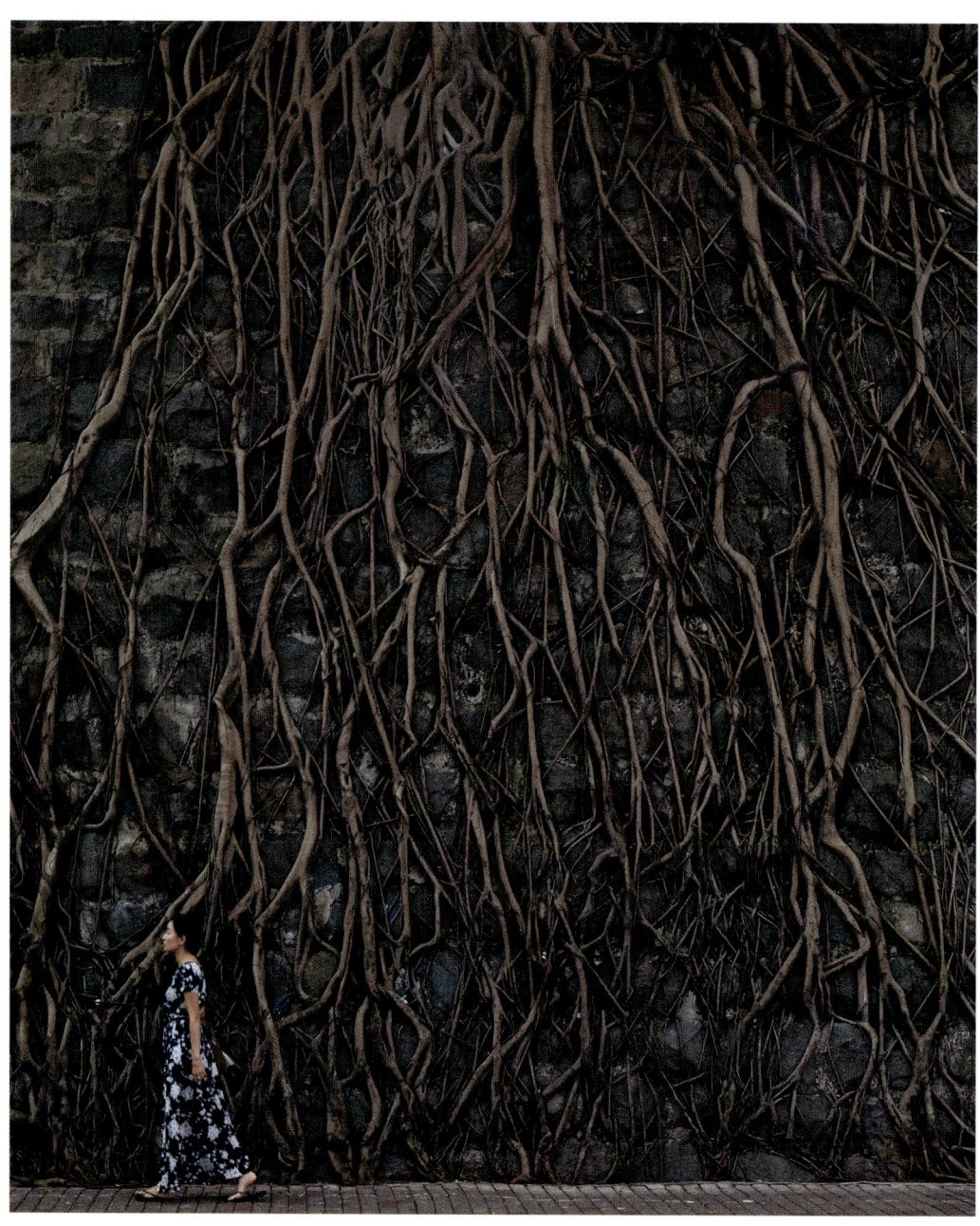

Life finds a way

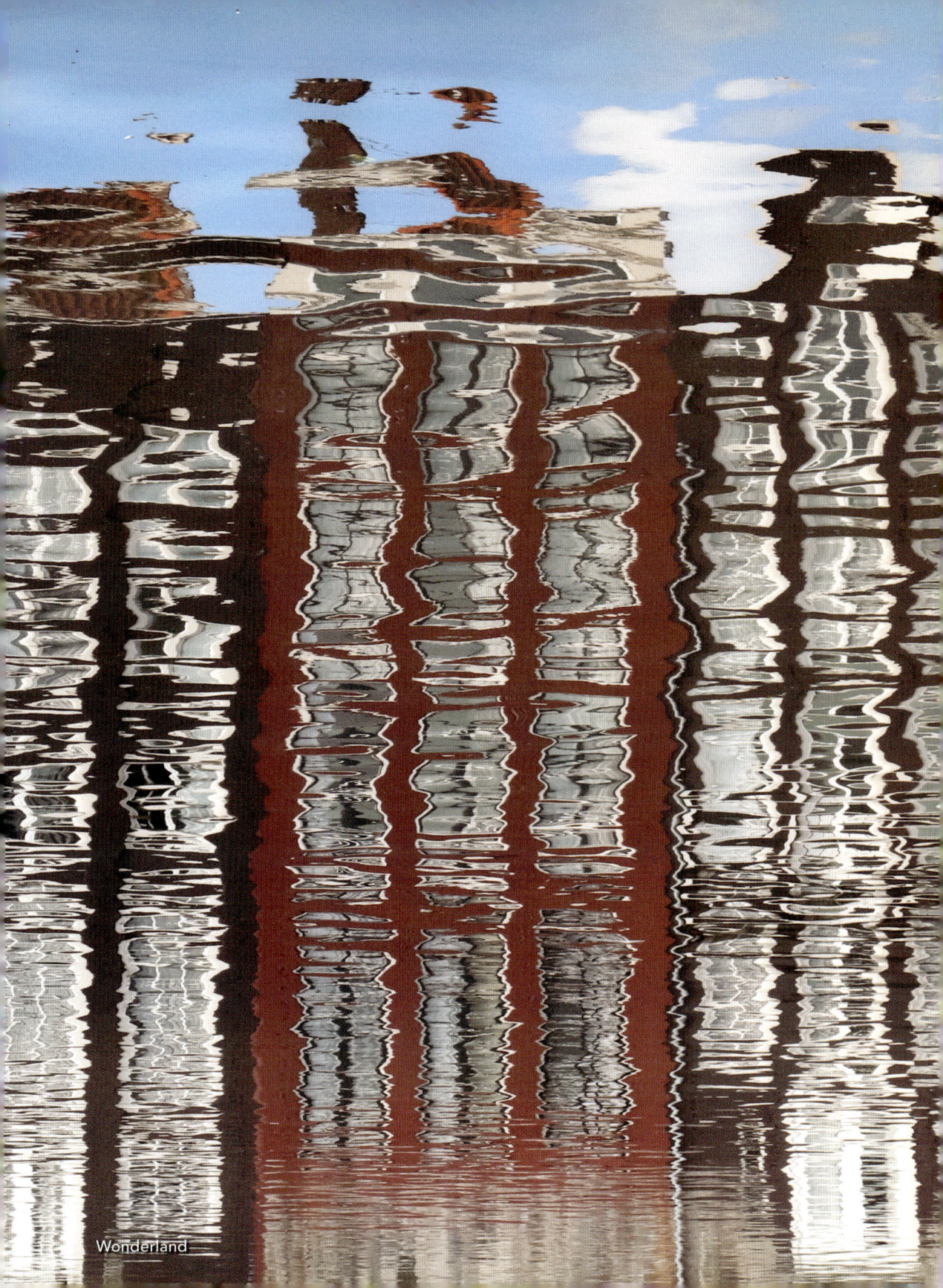
Wonderland

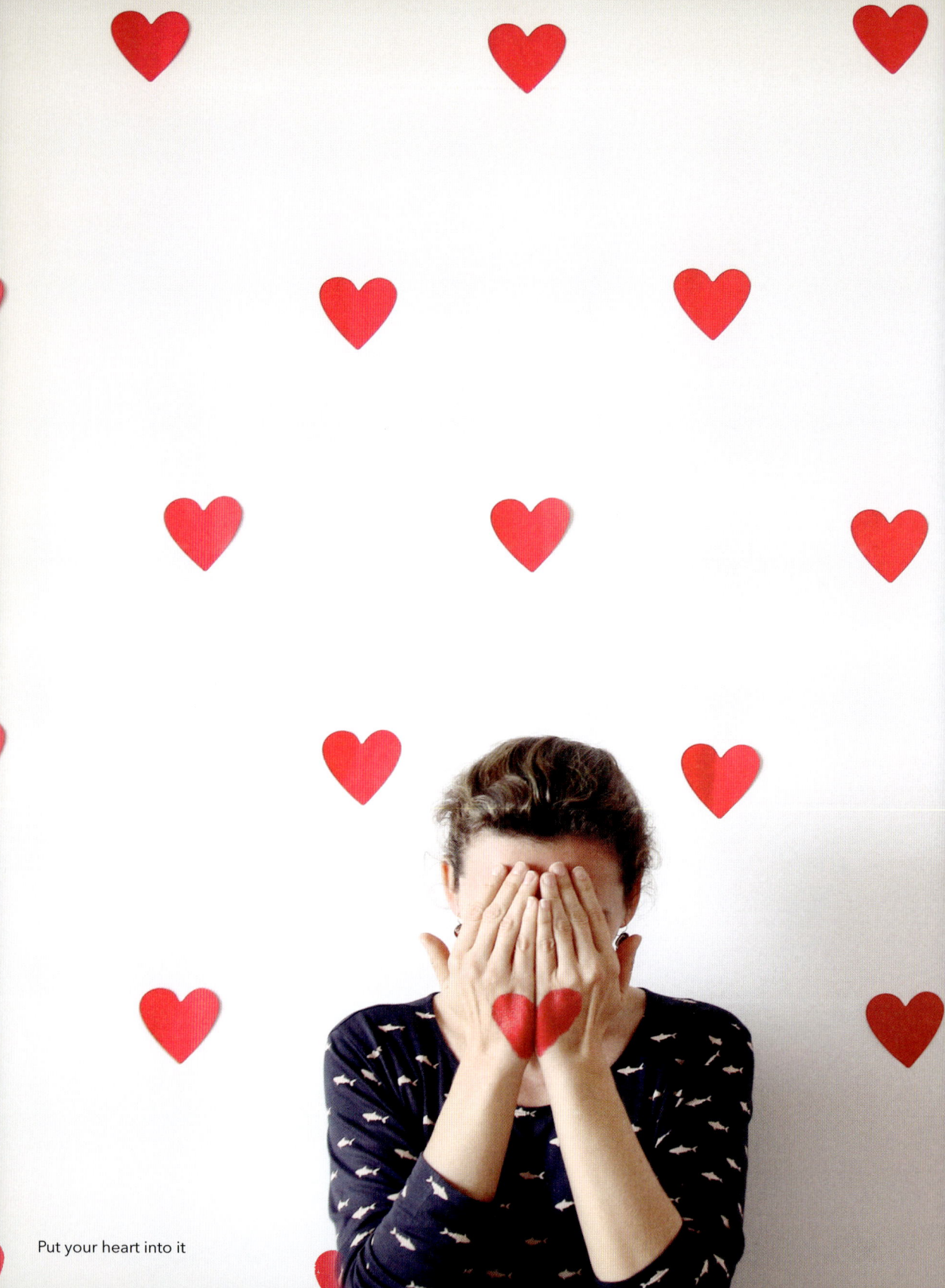

Put your heart into it

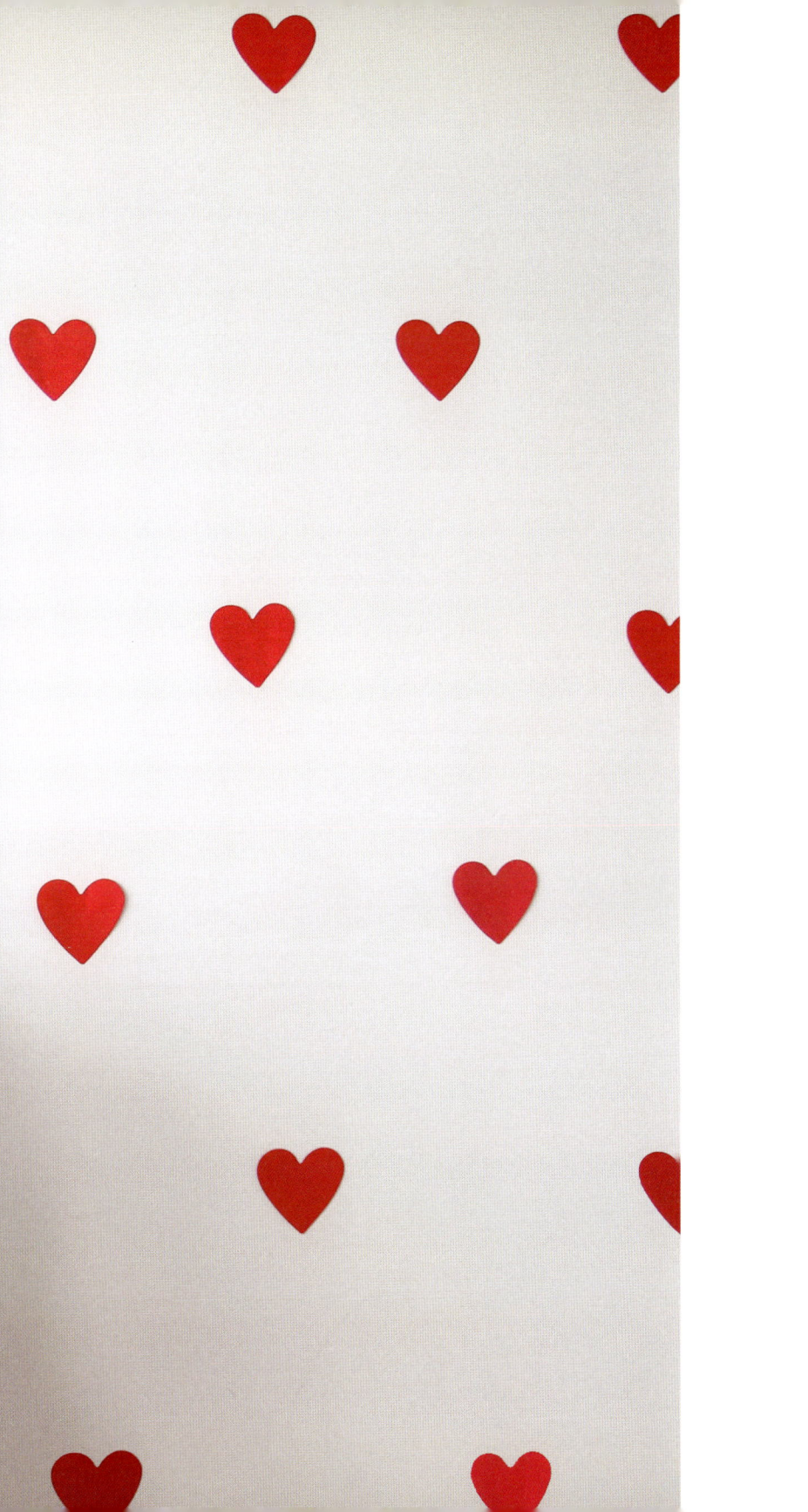

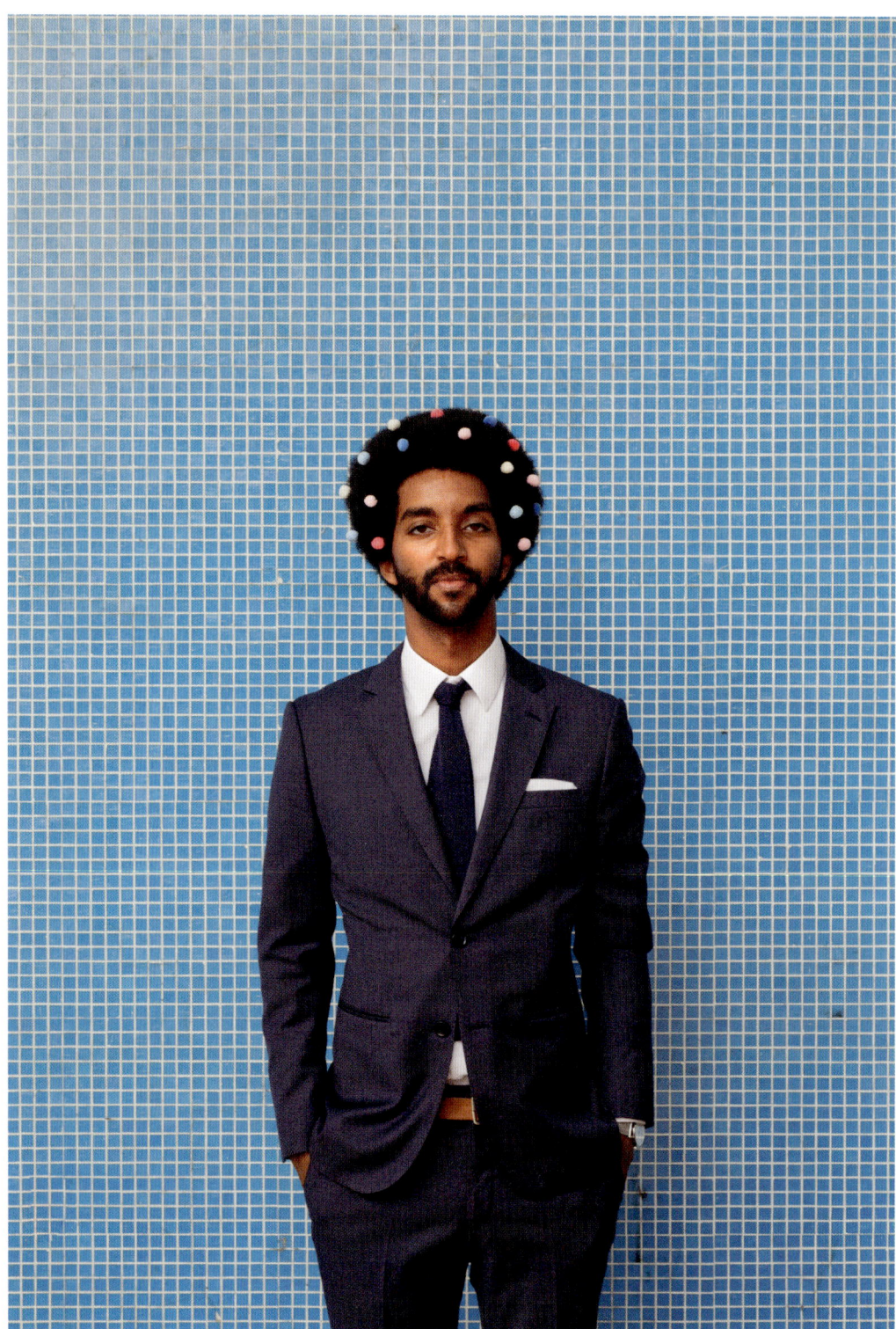

Sprinkles are for winners

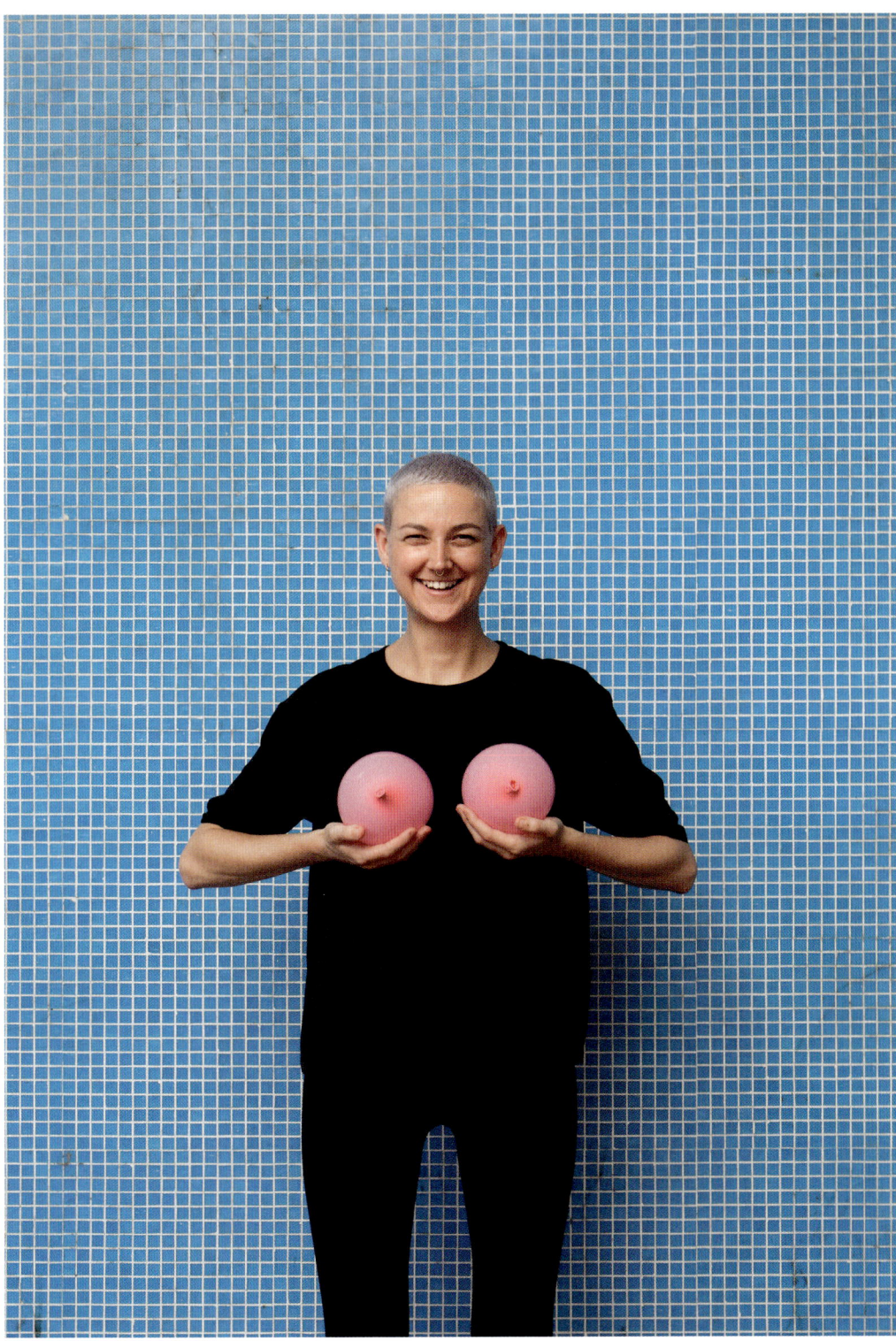

Define yourself

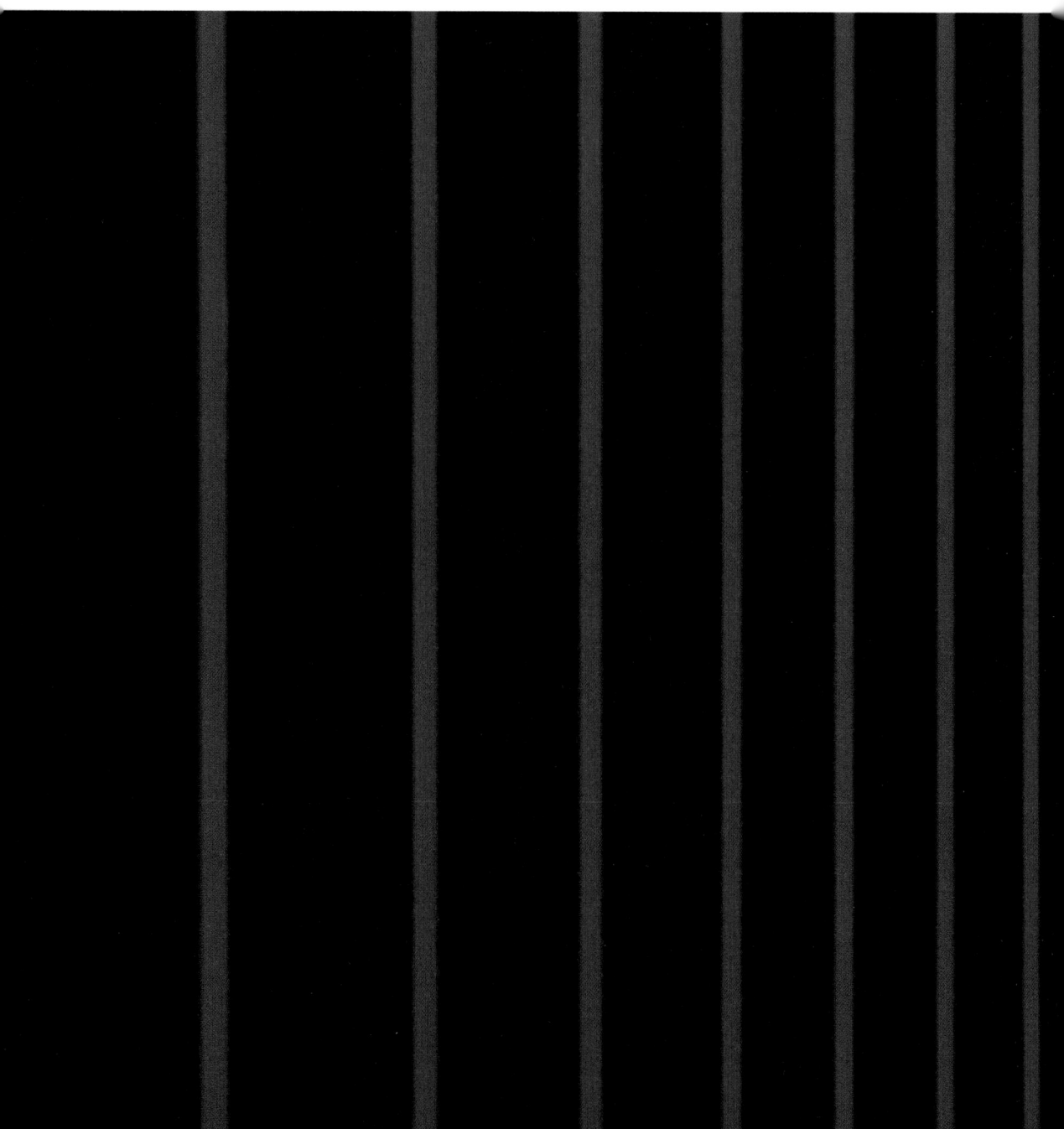

Cuckoo

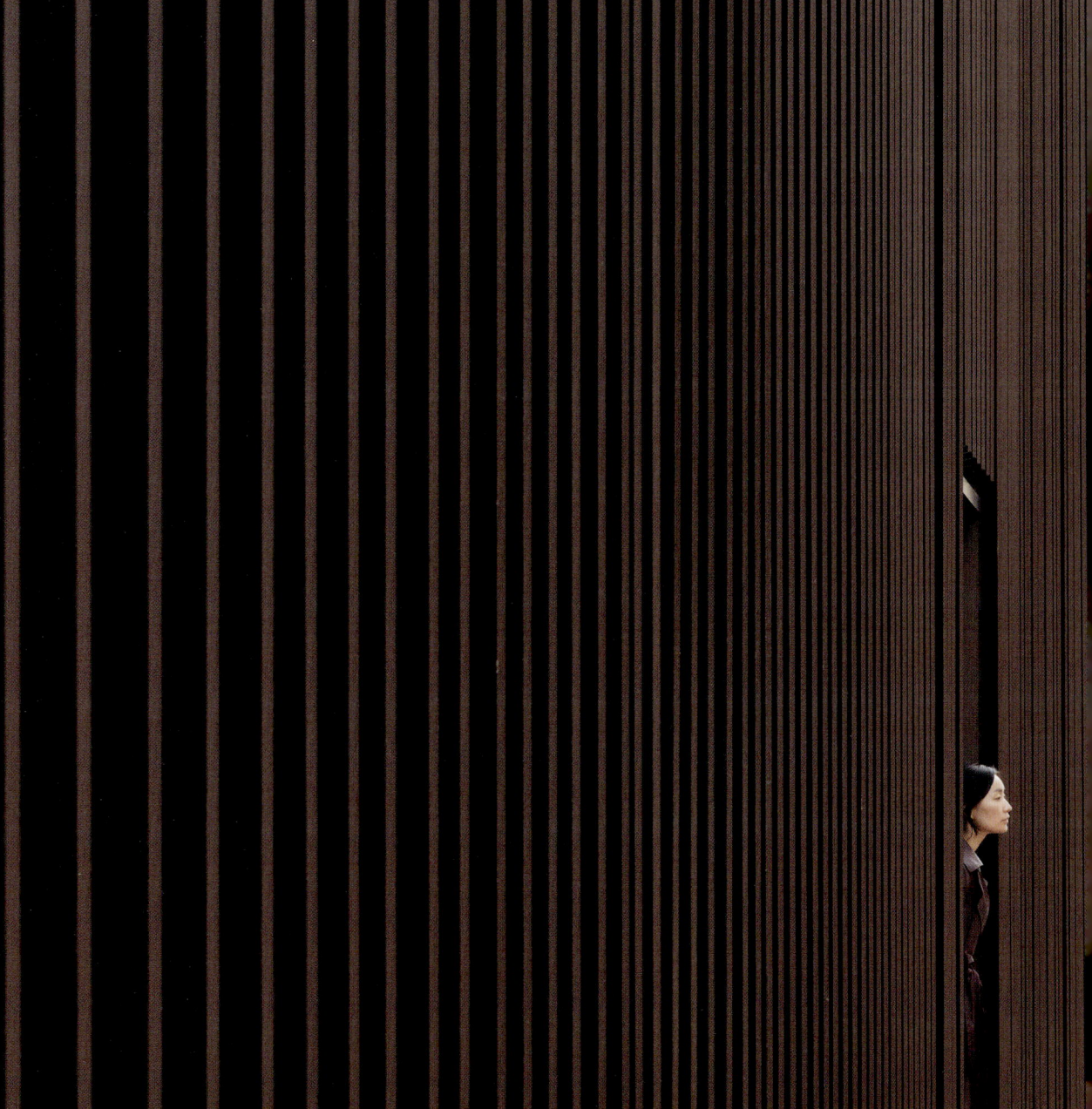

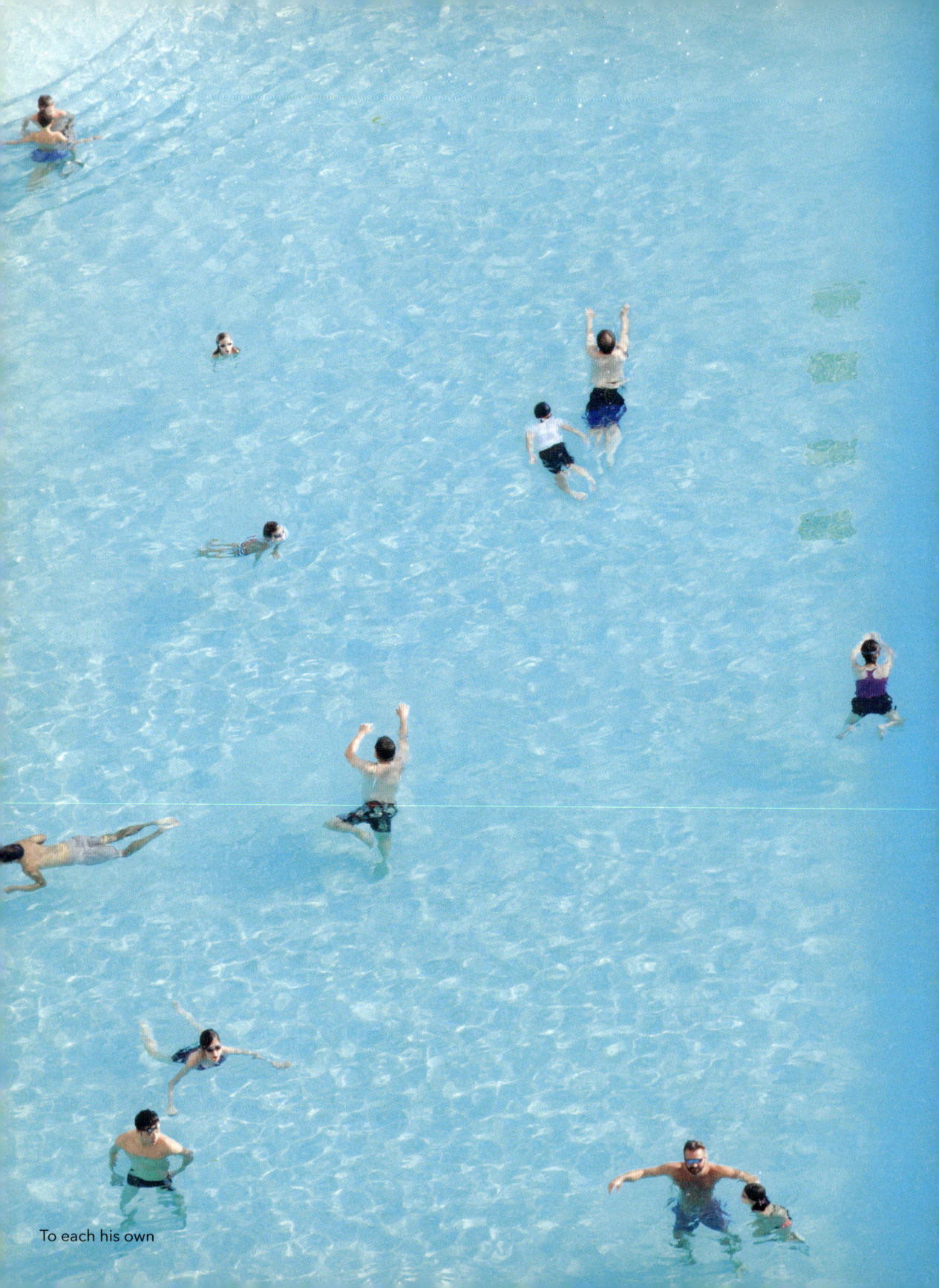

To each his own

Into my pocket

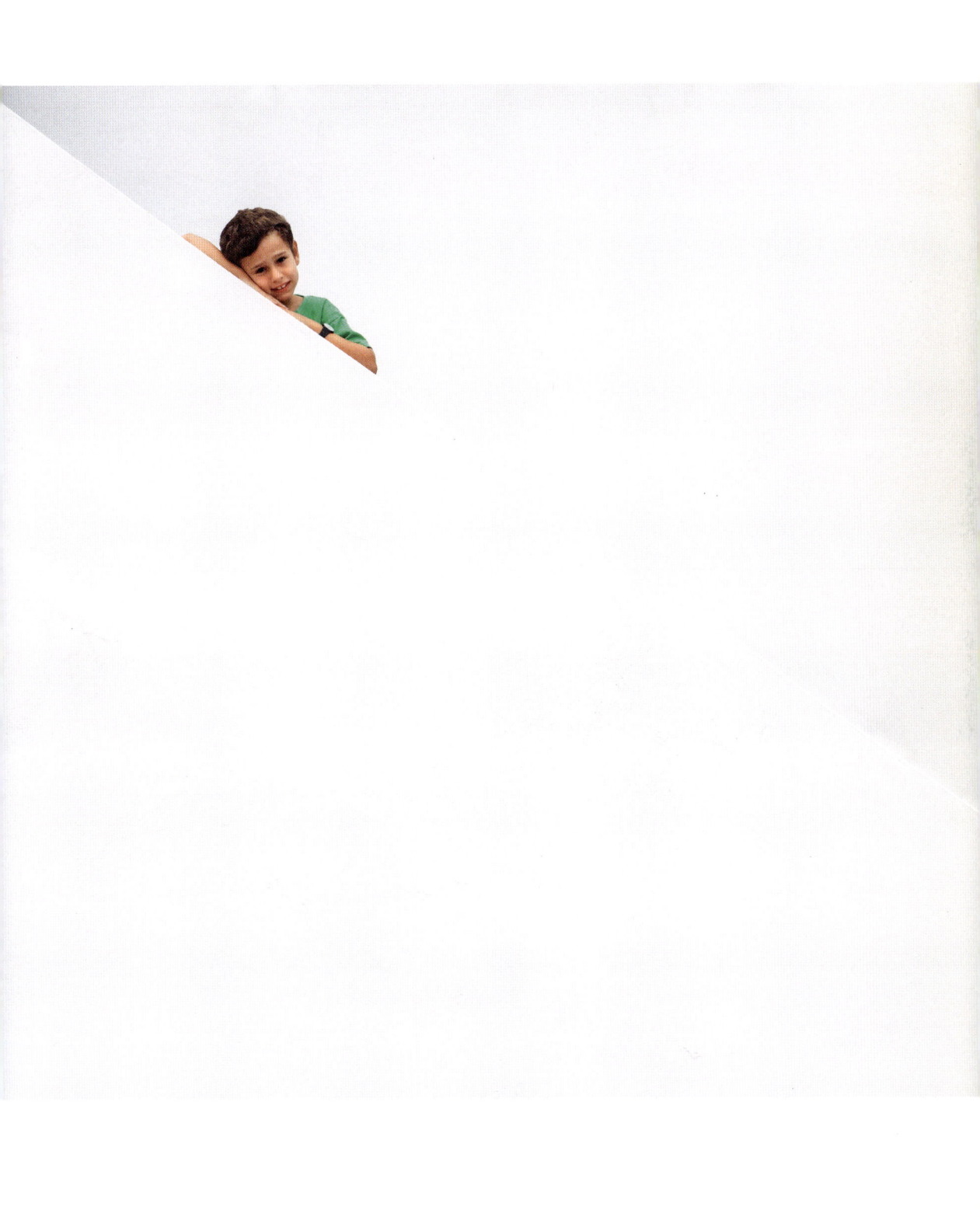

Please

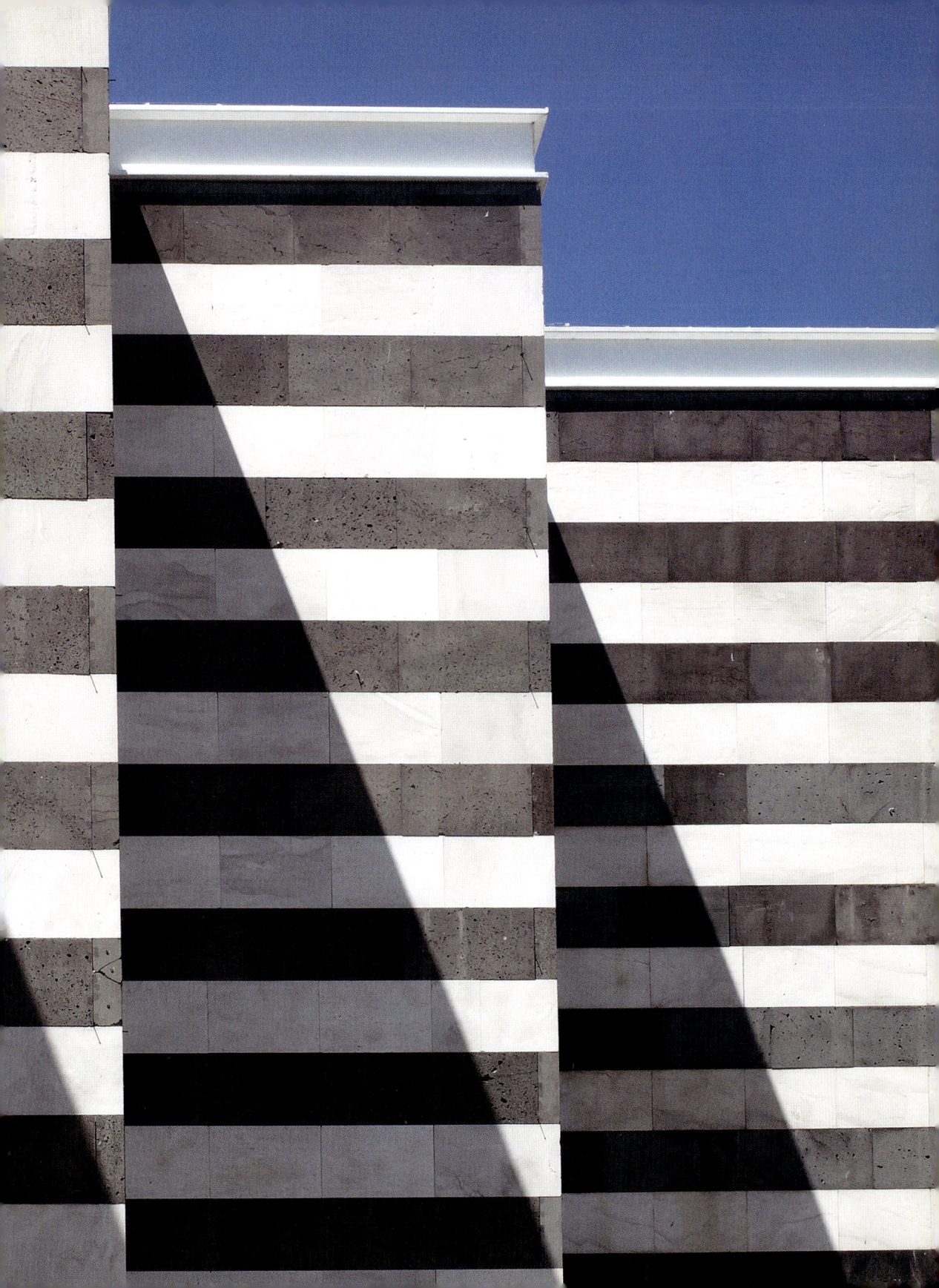

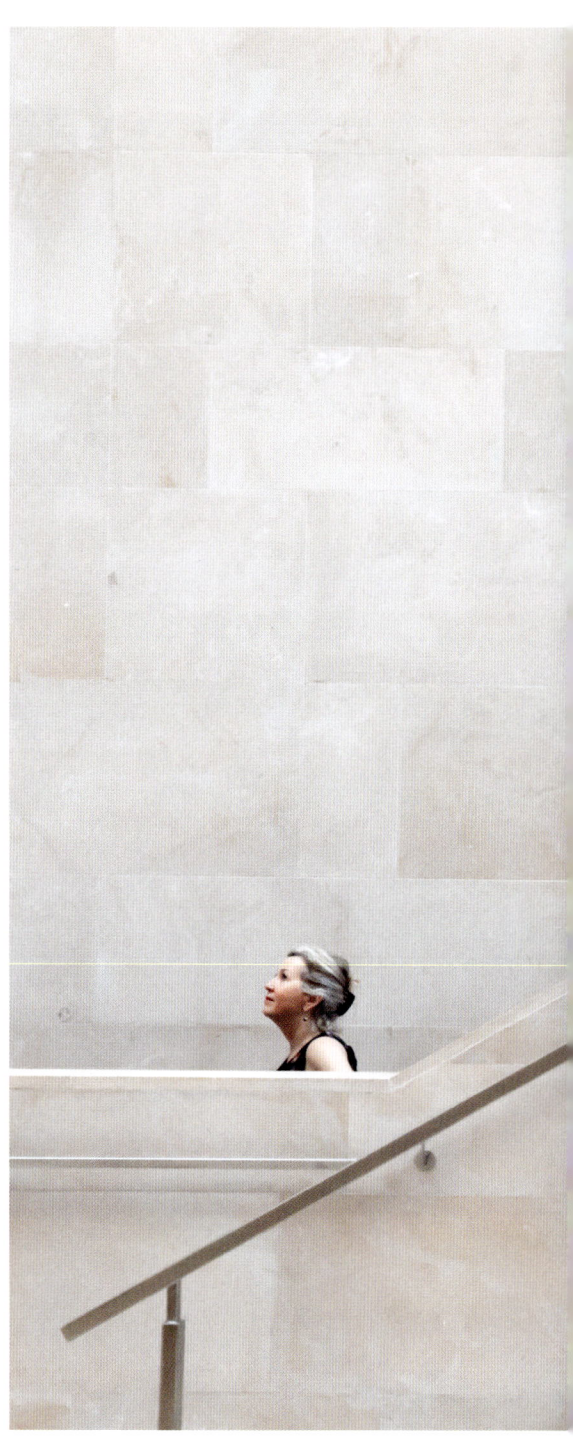

Knees and toes

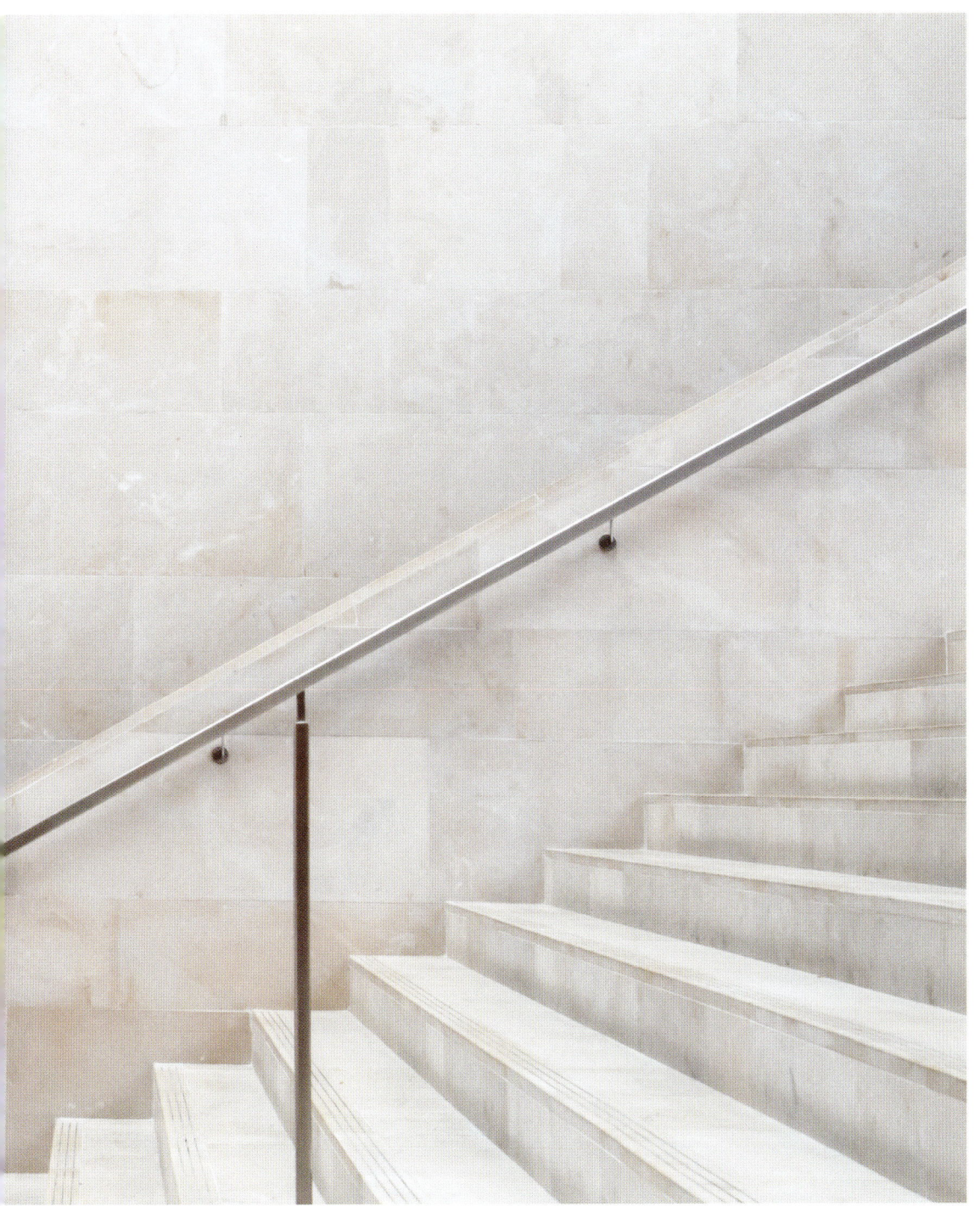

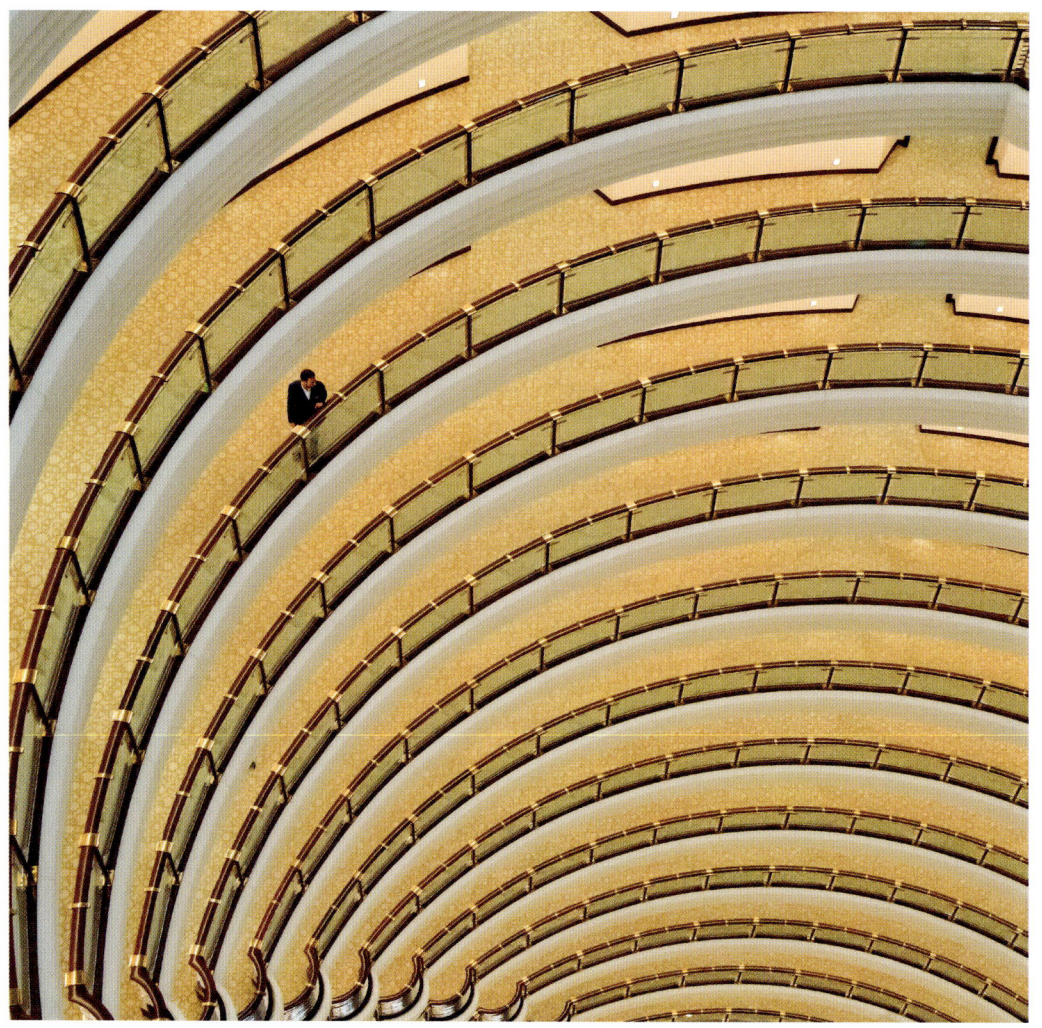

Vertigo

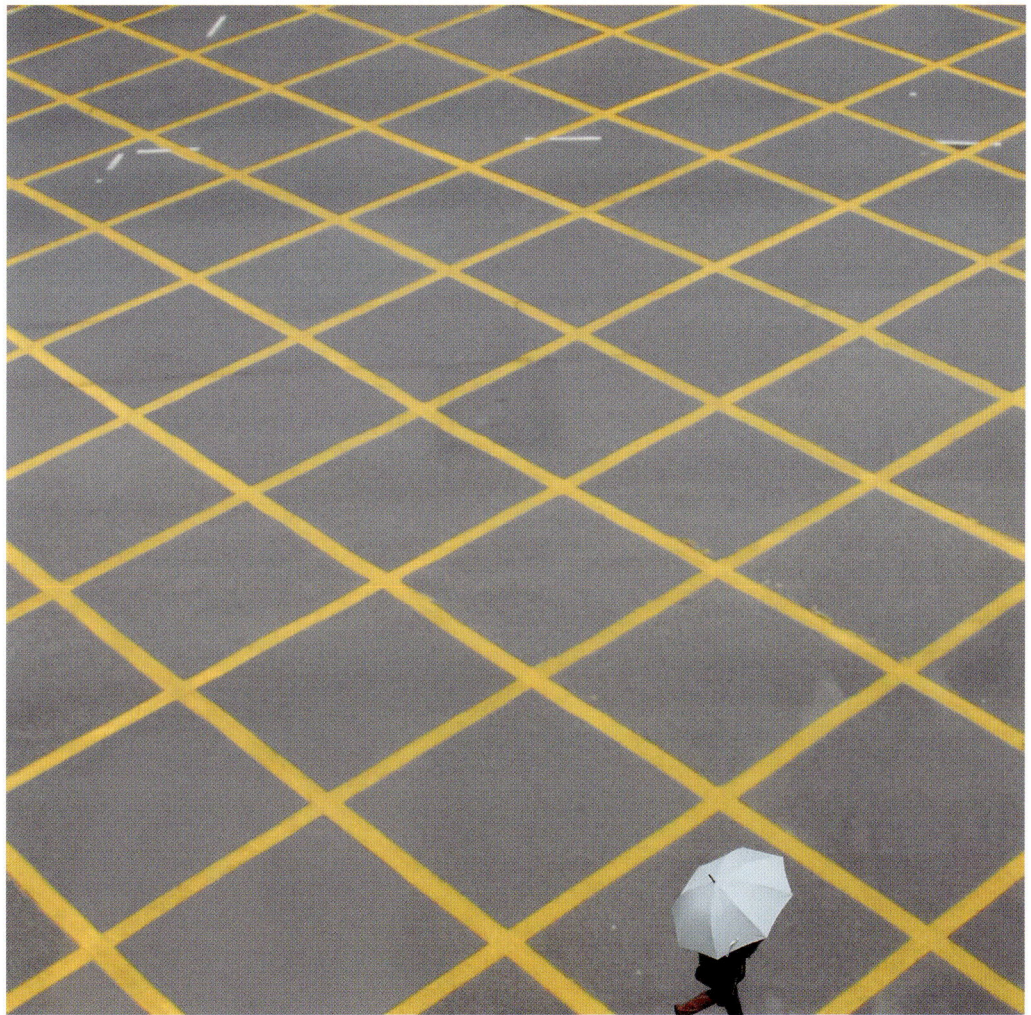

Pinball

Green was the silence

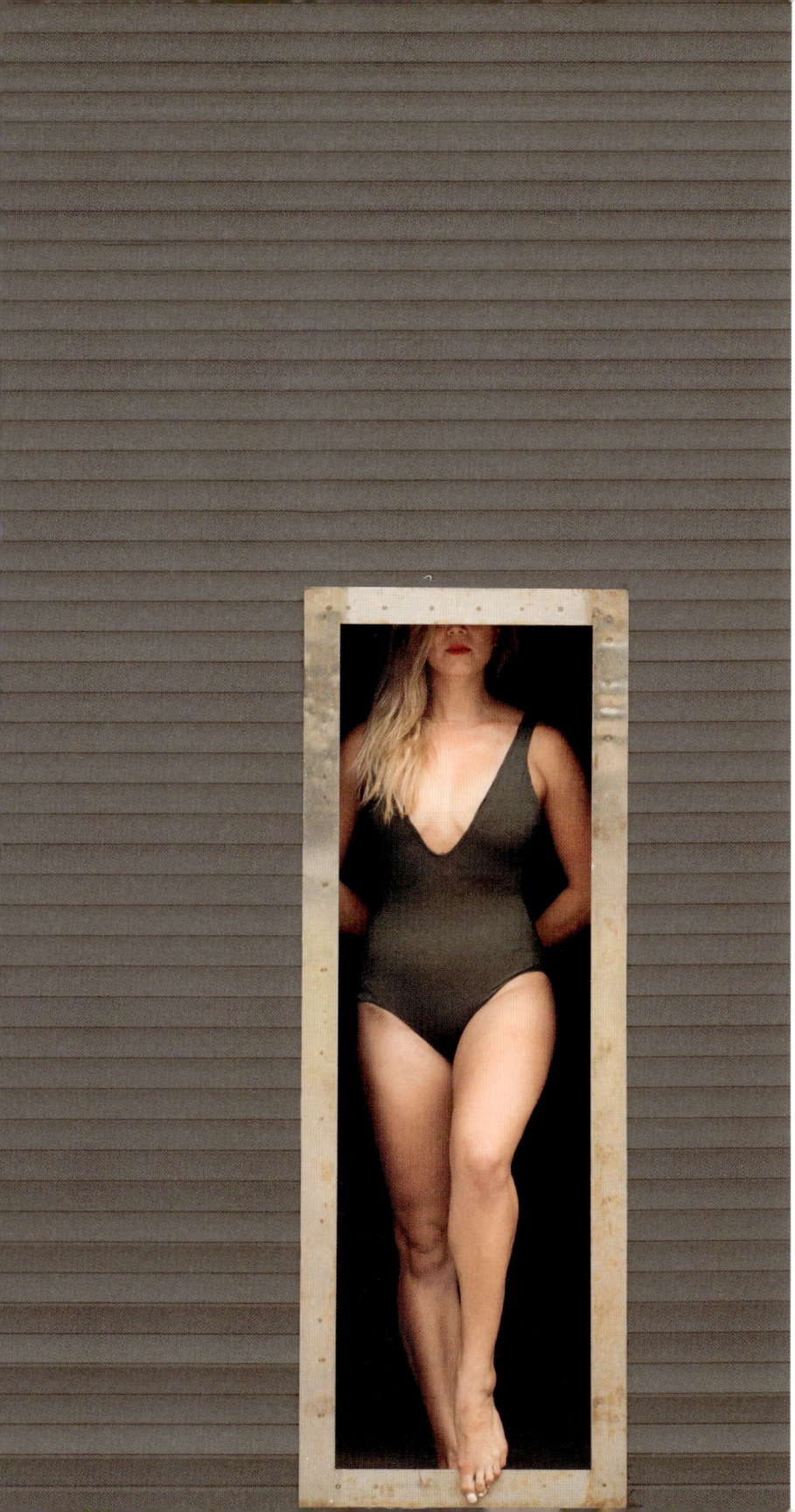

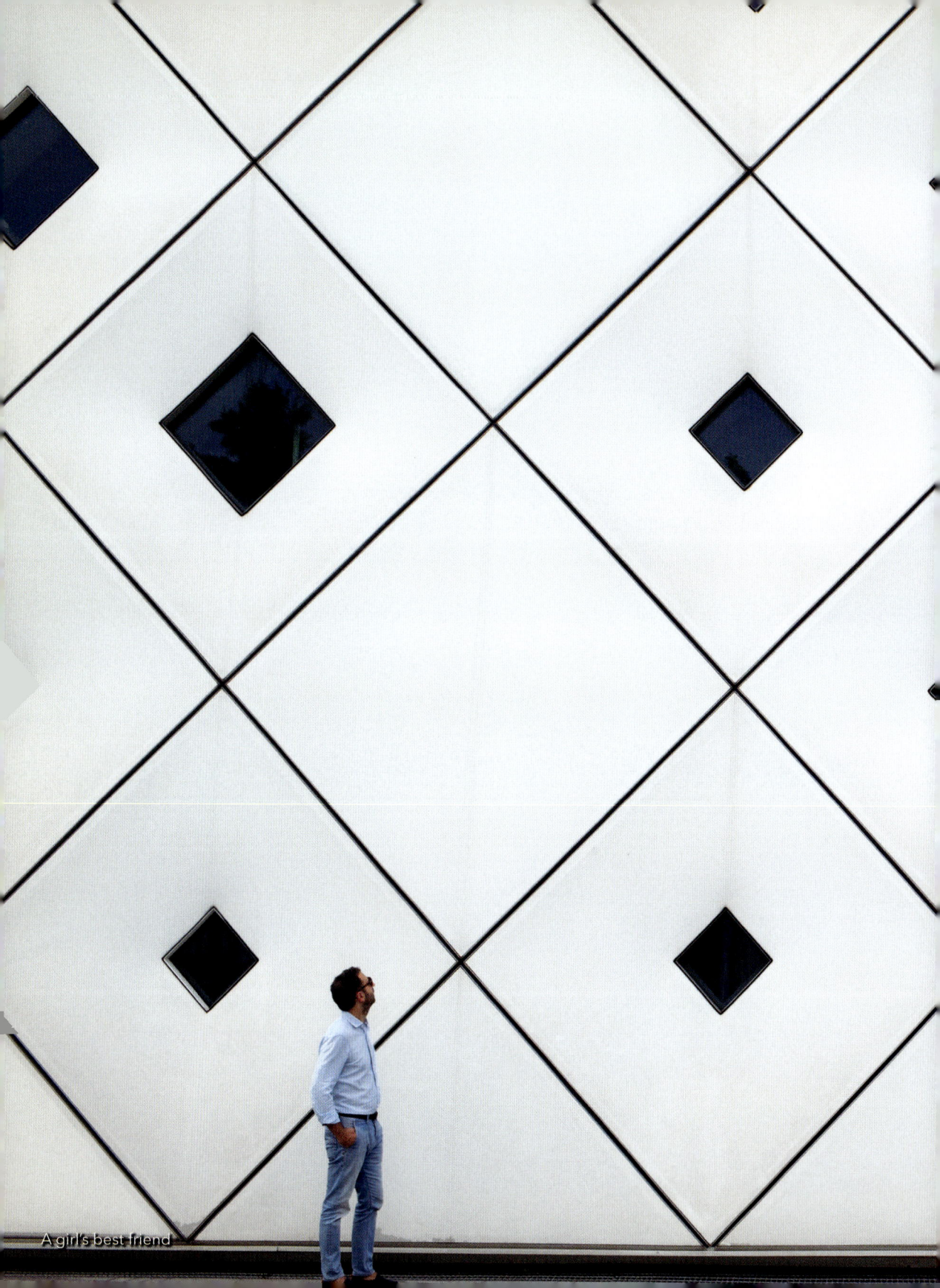

A girl's best friend

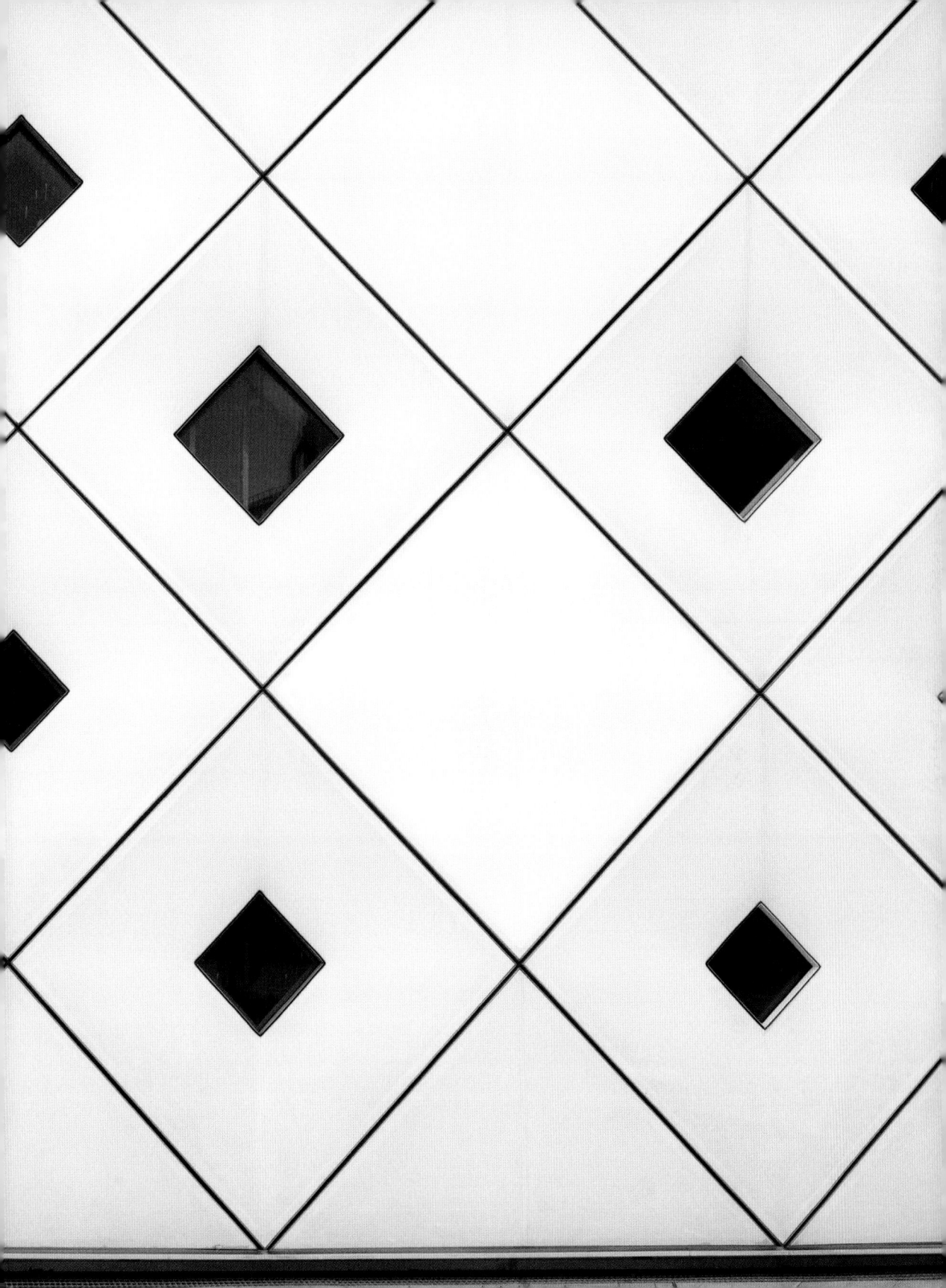

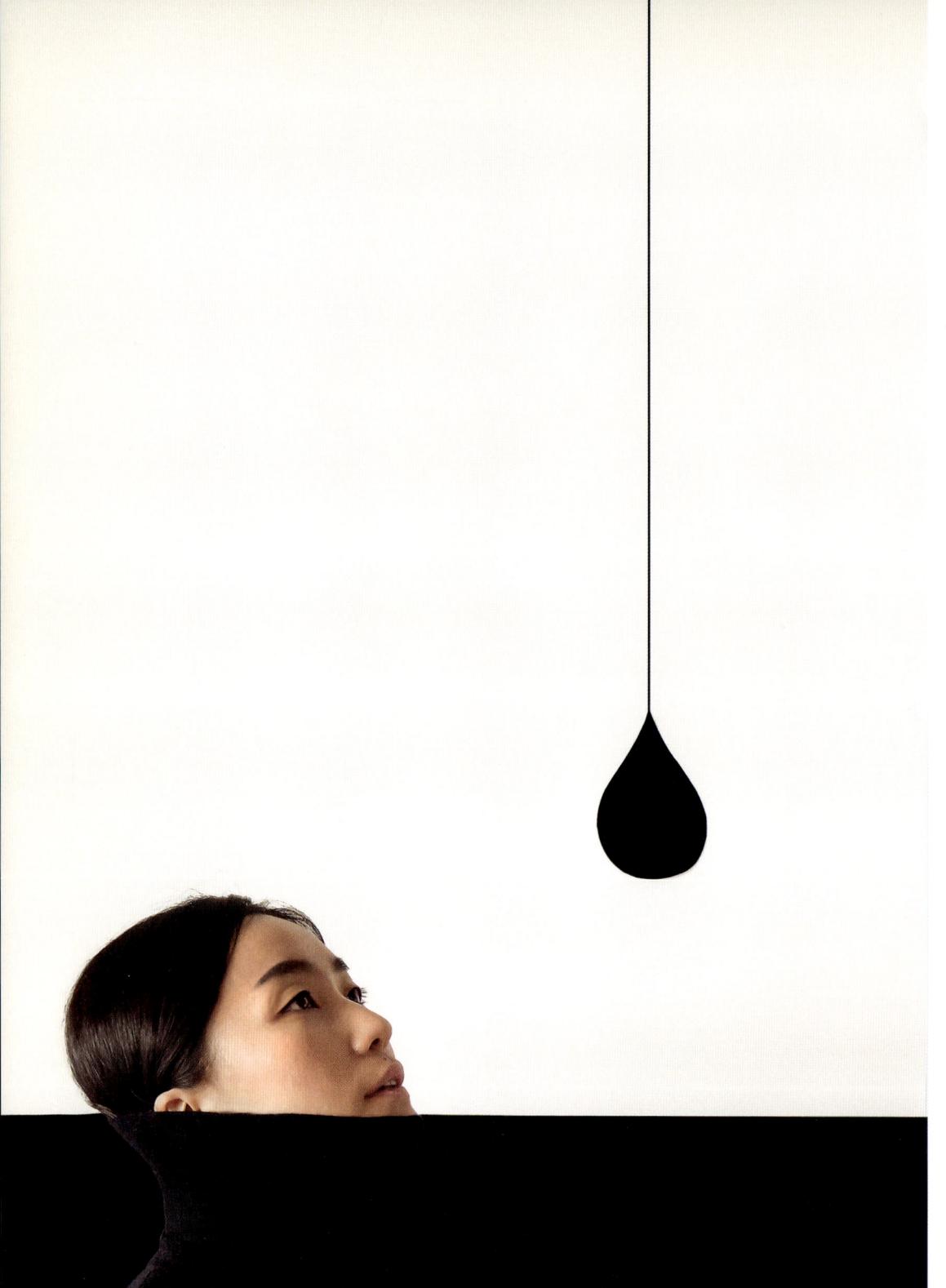

Ask the clouds to remember

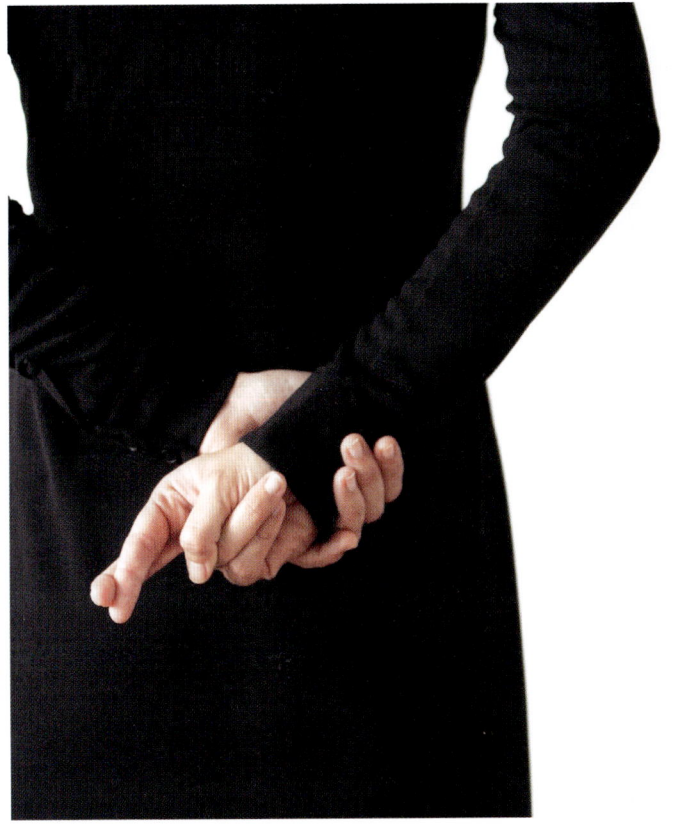

I swear

If cats could talk, they wouldn't

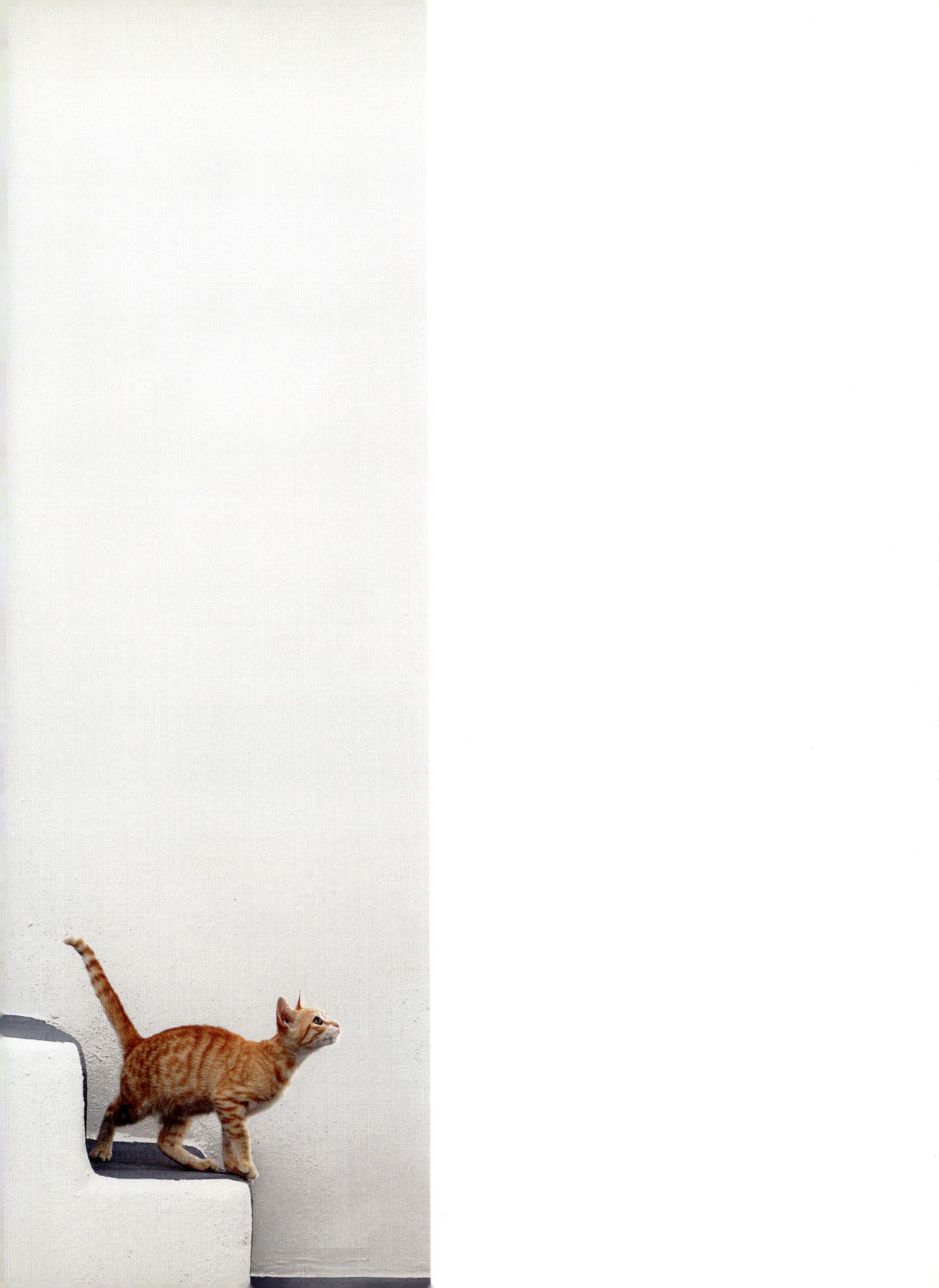

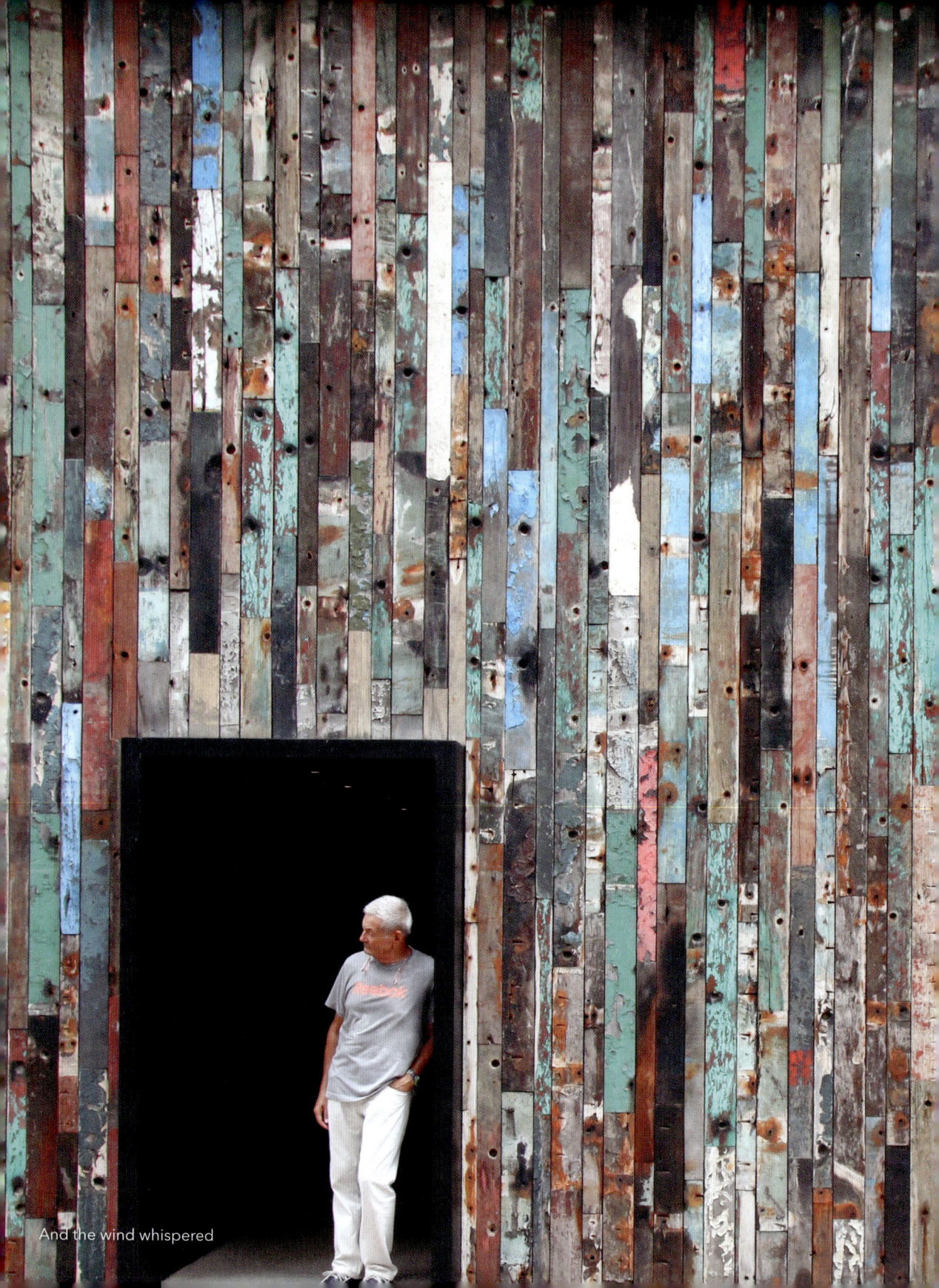

And the wind whispered

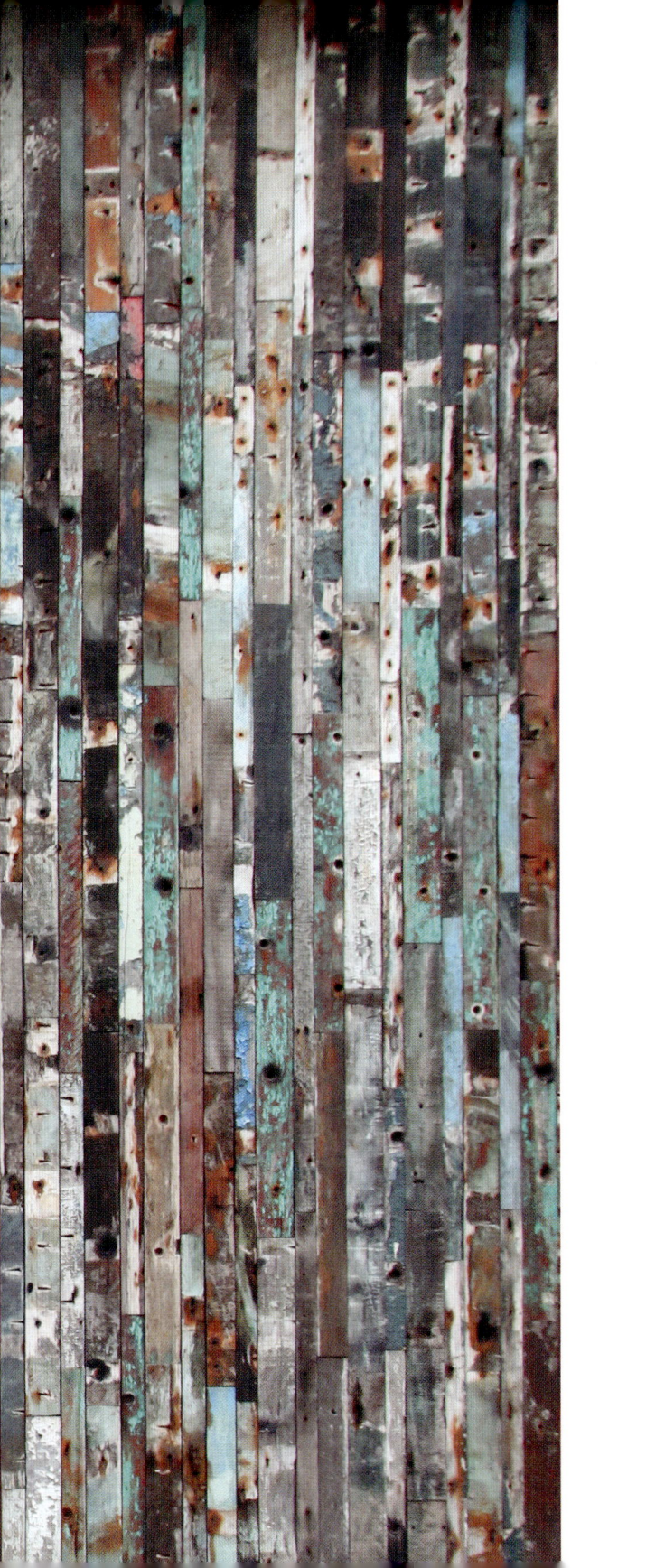

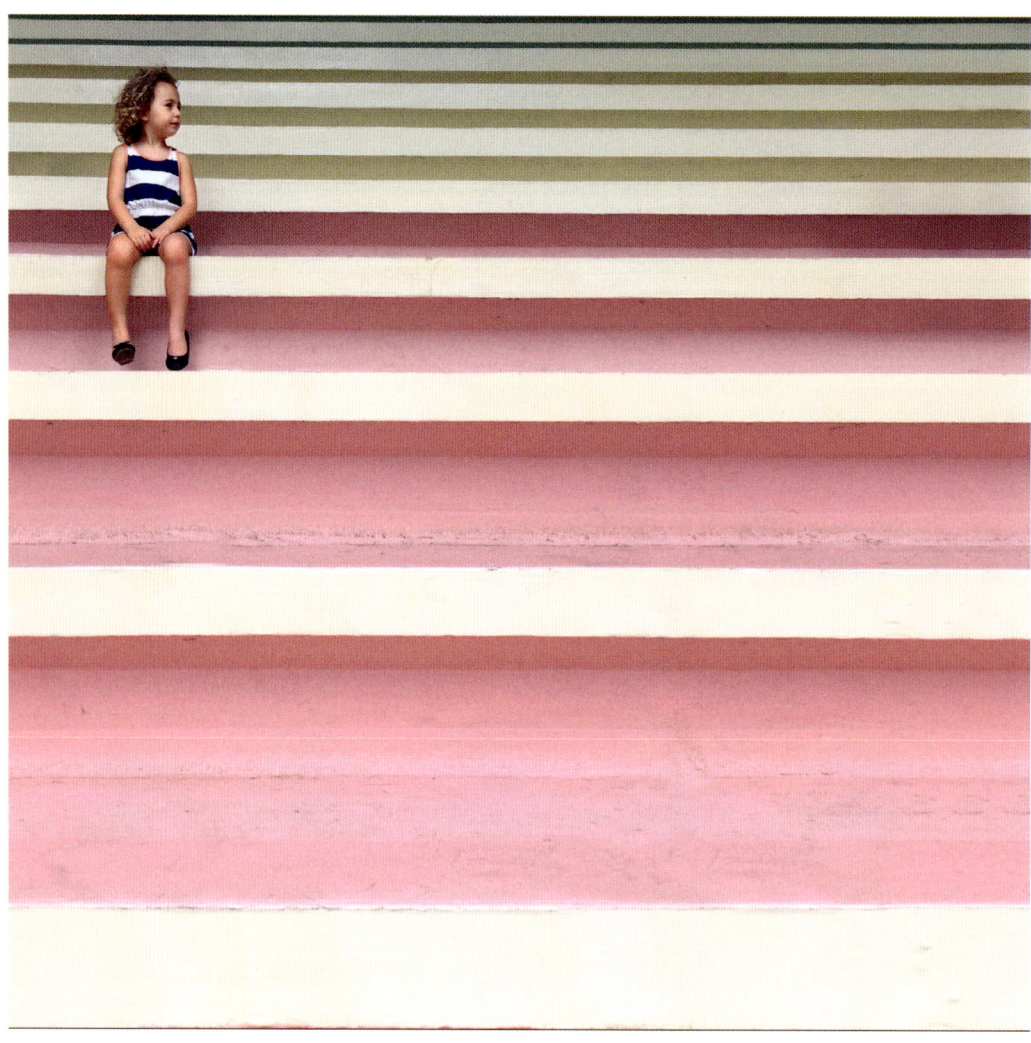

Oh baby, baby, it's a striped world

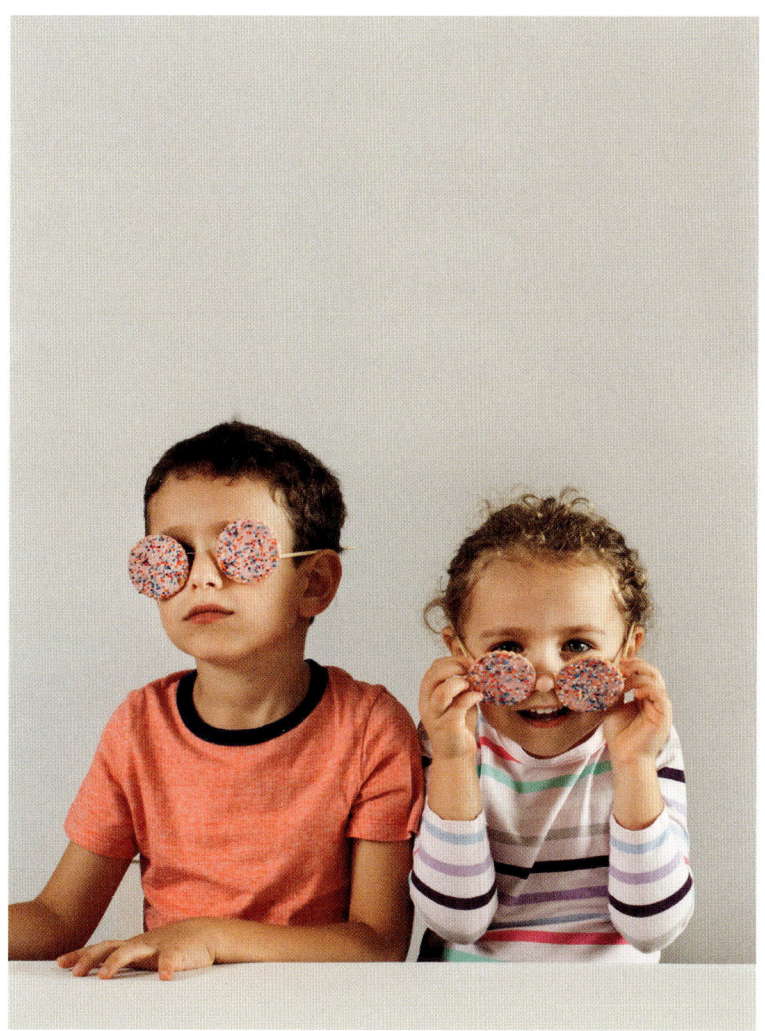

Too cool for school

# REALITY, CURATED

Published by New Heroes & Pioneers
Photography: Valentina Loffredo
Creative Direction: Francois Le Bled
Book Design: Jolien Brands
Copy Editing: Francois Le Bled

Printed and bound by Livonia (Latvia)
Legal deposit October 2020
ISBN 9789187815553

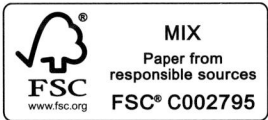

FSC
www.fsc.org
MIX
Paper from
responsible sources
FSC® C002795

Valentina Loffredo (born 1978) is an Italian artist, based in Hong Kong.
Her art practice begins in late 2013, when she starts experimenting
with photography and posts her images on Instagram. Her work
achieves international interest leading, in 2017, to a series of
solo and group exhibitions.
Her series "As for me, I'm very little" has been exhibited with solo shows
in Hong Kong and Milan and featured in "Personal Structures", collateral
event of the 57th Venice Art Biennale. Two of the photographs have been
exhibited by Sotheby's for the auction "Curated: turn it up".
Her second series, "Stillness", has been exhibited in PhotoFairs Shanghai
and with a solo show in Hong Kong.

**COLLECTIVE SHORTS**
*by* NHP PUBLISHING